Never Lick a Moving Blender!

Other books and tapes by Marvin Phillips

Books:
Don't Shoot: We May Both Be on the Same Side!
Booklet: *Let's Win Souls Now!*
Audio cassettes:
Coping with Stress!
Building Marriages That Last!
Feel Good about Yourself!
Video cassettes:
Coping with Stress!
Building Marriages That Last!

Available through Marvin Phillips (12000 E. 31st Street, Tulsa, Oklahoma, 74146-2001, 918-663-3000).

"The world needs a lot of Marvin Phillips!" (Zig Ziglar)

"A master speaker! His warm, encouraging personality radiates and inspires others to want to develop their potential. Written evaluations were equally enthusiastic. He is truly one of the best I have ever heard" (Kara Gae Wilson, Tulsa County Superintendent of Schools)

"Always leaves his audience feeling better about themselves and motivated to achieve. On a scale from one to ten, Mr. Phillips rates eleven!" (Barbara Wilson, Assistant to the Director, Special Education, Tulsa public schools)

Book Marvin Phillips to speak to your church, school, or company.

For more information call or write:
Marvin Phillips Seminars
12000 E. 31st Street
Tulsa, OK 74146-2001
(918) 663-3000

Never Lick a Moving Blender!

Humorous Insights
That Motivate
and Encourage

MARVIN PHILLIPS

HOWARD
PUBLISHING CO.

Our purpose at Howard Publishing is to:

- *Increase faith* in the hearts of growing Christians
- *Inspire holiness* in the lives of believers
- *Instill hope* in the hearts of struggling people everywhere

Because He's coming again!

Never Lick a Moving Blender!
© 1996 by Howard Publishing Co., Inc.
All rights reserved. Printed in the United States of America

Published by Howard Publishing Co., Inc.,
3117 North 7th Street, West Monroe, LA 71291-2227

00 01 02 03 04 05   10 9 8 7 6

Illustrated by Kristen Myers

ISBN 1-878990-58-6

Dedication

·❖·❖·❖·❖·❖·

This dedication is easy. It goes to my Peak of the Week class—that faithful group that comes every Wednesday night to hear one more lesson designed to peak their week. Some are regular members of Garnett Church of Christ where I have served as senior minister for the past twenty-six years. Others, and this number keeps growing, are those in my television audience who watched the program and then decided to become a part of the live class each week. We have a great time together. I think sometimes they motivate and encourage me more than I do them. We get a kick out of peaking each other's week. Here's to you, Peakers!

Contents

·❖·❖·❖·❖·❖·

CONTENTS

CONTENTS

CONTENTS

Foreword

·❖·❖·❖·❖·❖·

From the beginning Marvin said it could be done. Whatever the task, he thought we could do it. Whatever the mood against it, don't believe it. My initial introduction to this man was to observe his life, excitement, and joy. His charge was not for us to play dead to reality, but rather to wake up to potential.

All these years this man has prodded, promoted, and pushed for all of us to open our senses to certain, definite possibilities. I have watched him endure the "tough stuff" . . . and win. His talk has been in perfect cadence with his walk.

Marvin Phillips is at it again! He has put his heart in print that others might find reason to smile some, laugh a little, and hope a lot. *Never Lick a Moving Blender!* is a painfully funny thought. And, the more one thinks about it, the more the practical application surfaces.

A series of one stirring provocation after another comes to the reader from these pages. Light-hearted humor begins to soak the heart. And then? A realization begins to sweep across the mind saying things like, "Oh no, that's the way *I* am" or "Hey, this guy's right." *Never Lick a Moving Blender!* is more than good advice . . . it's great medicine.

This work is a comic strip put into delightful word pictures. Some of them you can envision. Others you will feel. Some you may duck as they narrowly miss. Quips are sometimes quick. Other stories inspire. But there is something even more unique. There seems to be a new awareness regarding our own surroundings, as if we had put on 3-D glasses. We may laugh at ourselves a little. For certain, we will see ourselves a lot.

If you need a hearty change of pace, don't switch brands of coffee. Relax a bit. With ease, begin to read. *Never Lick a Moving Blender!* will cause you to get serious about not taking everything that goes on too seriously!

Terry Rush
Tulsa, Oklahoma

Preface

This book is really a third collection of stuff I do in my Wednesday "Peak of the Week" classes. Three of my five books have shared these weekly encouragement infusions. The previous two were, *You Can't Fly to Heaven in a Straight Line* and *Put Peak in Your Week.*

My third book, *The Joy Factor of Church Growth,* offers sermons on evangelism and church growth. It came from a course I teach each September at Kentucky Christian College in Grayson, Kentucky. The fourth book was on fellowship—*Don't Shoot: We May Both Be on the Same Side.*

With *Never Lick a Moving Blender!* I am returning to my roots. Joy, happiness, success, and encouragement are my favorite stuff.

The Peak of the Week class (and now television series) is an idea that clicked. It worked. Nonmembers started attending. Now clearly a third of my weekly audience is composed of those who are not members of the Garnett Church. The television audience has appreciated my boots-and-bluejeans approach, and down-to-earth style.

PREFACE

Everywhere I go, people stop me to say they watch and enjoy Peak of the Week! Many who are now dedicated Christians got their start in this nonthreatening environment. What began as a thirteen-week experiment has now continued over ten years. Without a doubt, more books will be forthcoming from the Peak of the Week series.

Elsewhere in the book is a page that tells you where to get the other books and tapes I've done and how to arrange for me to speak to your church, school, or company.

Thanks for reading this one. I'll be rewarded if you like it and are motivated to greater enjoyment of life and service to God and his cause. I hope it not only "peaks your week" but your whole life and eternity as well.

Acknowledgments

·❖·❖·❖·❖·❖·

To borrow an old Winston Churchill expression, "Never has one man owed so much to so many!" I am grateful to the members of the Garnett Church of Christ who have loved me and encouraged me in my local ministry, my travels, and my writing. I thank Linna Clinton, my secretary, who proofread the chapters and offered suggestions for changes, for putting up with me when my attitude was bad when I was pressed because of time deadlines. You see I wrote this book in the months following cancer surgery. It made a difference in my stamina and sometimes my concentration.

I thank my peak audience, both live and television. They have been overwhelming in their enthusiasm for the class, the television show, and the books that came out of it.

Last of all, I thank my God for his grace to a stumbling, fumbling preacher. He has allowed me to travel all over the world spreading the Good News about Jesus. And he has allowed me to preach locally, for twenty-six years, to one of the greatest audiences any man has ever addressed.

I am a very blessed man!

The difference between
"try" and "triumph"
is just a little "umph!"

❖·❖·❖·❖·❖

"What the mind of man
can conceive
and believe
his life can achieve."

He had the most pitiful expression on his face you ever saw. I'm talking about Grimm—Mother Goose's dog— from the comic strip by the same name. He's a pitiful look- ing thing anyway. He's always getting into trouble— drinking from the toilet, hunting lunch in a garbage can, and other deplorables.

This time he went too far, and the picture told the whole story. Most comic strips have three or four frames. Today there was only one. Grimm was at the far left. The blender was at the far right. Grimm's tongue stretched the full dis- tance between, caught in a tangled mess around the blades of that blender. The caption said it all. It preached the ser- mon and gave this advice: "Never lick a moving blender!"

How many times have you made Grimm's mistake? You can follow his thought process as he spots that blender at work. Looks good. Smells right. Intent harmless. But the effort wasn't worth the pain.

Lots of things in life are like that. Kids disobey their parents. They don't really mean any harm; they're just having a little fun. They don't want to hurt anyone, but disobedience gets to be a habit. Before long it seeps into the classroom. It extends to the community. A little theft occurs here and there. Looks okay. Smells right. Just seems like a little fun that brings a few kicks. Nobody really gets hurt.

We all expect to be the exception to the rule, but what we expect and what we get are sometimes vastly different. Our tongues get caught in the blenders of life. There's a bunch of pain we hadn't counted on. We become one more statistic proving the old adage that "crime does not pay!"

Don't Cut Off Your Nose to Spite Your Face

There are lots of sayings that call to us—clichés that click, pointers that really point somewhere. Here's another one: "Don't cut off your nose to spite your face." It means don't retaliate when it will hurt you more than it will help the situation.

Grudges always hurt the "grudger" more than the "grudgee."

Remember the story? One guy holds his finger against a brick wall. He says to his friend, "Hit my finger." Of course he moves his finger at the last minute and the friend's fist hits hard, rough bricks, skinning his knuckles. To get revenge, the friend says, "See if you can hit this." And he holds his forefinger against his own nose. Pow!

You wouldn't be so dumb would you? But you might hold a grudge against someone.

You might say, "I'll get you back if it's the last thing I ever do!"

Grudges always hurt the "grudger" more than the "grudgee." Our attempts at revenge hurt us more than they help. You stay away from the family reunion because someone will be there who has done you wrong. You quit church because someone hurt you or because you didn't agree with some decision that was made.

Never give anyone the power to affect the peace and harmony of your life. Staying away from that reunion can affect scores of people. Damage may be done for years to come.

Quitting the church because of something someone else did is a lot like getting mad at the dog and kicking the cat. The church belongs to Jesus. He died for it. He bought it with his blood. Don't let anyone affect your response to the amazing grace of the cross.

Don't Drown Your Sorrows in Alcohol!

Your problems seem insurmountable. You don't think you can go on. You want to throw up your hands and throw in the towel. You've had it. You're at the end of your rope; so you head for the bottle.

Your intentions are good. You need the escape. Problems look different through the bottom of a whiskey bottle. If you drink enough, hey, problems will disappear. Everything will be different. But you can't drown your sorrows. They float! And the result won't be worth it.

you can't drown your sorrows. They float!

When you wake up from that drunken stupor, your problems will still be there, only they will have multiplied. Where is my car? Does it have all the fenders? What am I doing in this

5

room? This bed? Who is this woman? What am I going to do now?

The question is not, "Where can I run?" The questions ought to be, "How can I fix this? How can I get my job back? How can I hold my marriage together? Lord, what will you have me do?"

Everything is based on cause and effect. Each decision causes a specific result. We've got to face that. It's like the light switch on the wall. You can't switch it off and expect the light to come on. "There is a way that seems right to a man, but in the end it leads to death" (Proverbs 14:12).

If You Want Strawberries, Don't Plant Broccoli

We all want the same outcome—to be happy and to end up with a reasonable measure of health, wealth, and happiness. "Do not be deceived: God cannot be mocked. A man reaps what he sows" (Galatians 6:7). Broccoli seeds won't produce strawberries.

Seeds are strange little things—they teach us a lot about life. They don't grow unless they are planted. And good news: we can plant what we want. If we want watermelons, we plant watermelon seed. If we want strawberries, we've got to plant strawberries. The problem is that some people want to plant one thing and reap another. We want one result, but we do what brings the opposite result. We want to plant immorality and reap respectability. We want to plant dishonesty and reap a reputation of integrity. It simply doesn't work that way.

And seeds are powerful. I have a 175-foot driveway. Every year I battle grass that grows right up through the asphalt. It's great to know that if the right seeds are planted in the right place, you'll get the desired result.

It's also true with life. We can plant whatever we choose, from our attitudes, to our reactions, to our responses. Don't plant bitterness and expect to reap tenderness. Don't neglect your family today and expect them to lovingly gather around you in your later years. Don't dissipate your body with alcohol and drugs and expect the joys of good health when you grow old. "You may be sure that your sin will find you out" (Numbers 32:23).

It doesn't matter who the planter is. It's a law of sowing and reaping. Once we learn this fantastic principle, we can decide what we want. Then we plant the words, decisions, and actions that are necessary. The end result should be what we wanted in the first place.

Don't Try to Leap a Chasm in Two Jumps

It was obviously his first airplane ride. We were enroute from Los Angeles to Honolulu. In his nervousness he asked the flight attendant, "Miss, is this a nonstop flight?" With a knowing smile she replied, "I sure hope so."

Leaping a chasm in two jumps is impossible, and so is living without love. But some attempt the impossible anyway. They are afraid to love, afraid they'll be hurt. They've been hurt before; so, now they're "once burned, twice shy." They don't want to repeat the experience; so they choose to keep their feelings to themselves. They choose not to express their love in words or actions because they think they are safer that way.

But the end result is toughness on the outside and rot on the inside. Sure love is vulnerable. Sure you can get hurt if you love. But the alternative is not worth it. Living without love is not living at all.

Some attempt another impossible task—they try to live without giving. Someone has said there are three philosophies about your possessions:

What's mine is mine and you can't have it!
What's yours is mine if I can get it!
What's mine is yours if you need it!

The first two don't lead anywhere worthwhile.

The first Christians had the right philosophy. "They gave to anyone as he had need" (Acts 2:45). "No one claimed that any of his possessions was his own, but they shared everything they had" (Acts 4:32).

Jesus taught, "Give, and it will be given to you. A good measure, pressed down, shaken together and running over, will be poured into your lap. For with the measure you use, it will be measured to you" (Luke 6:38).

Preachers sometimes misunderstand this verse. They see the word give and immediately pass the collection plates. But the word *money* is not in that verse. In fact, it doesn't appear anywhere in the chapter. It's a principle. It applies to everything.

Do you want trouble? Give it and you'll get plenty of it back. Do you want love and affection, good relationships, and a good marriage? Do you want health, wealth, and happiness? The verse says "give and it will be given you." And the return will be "a good measure, pressed down, shaken together and running over."

This is especially true in marriage. Two simple things are of vital importance for a happy, successful marriage: study your mate, and give your mate everything he or she needs.

We are really simple creatures. Write down what it takes to please you. What do you need from your mate? You'll write things like, "I need to be loved," "I need affection," "I need to feel needed," "I want to feel a part of his life." Before you have written five things, they will already be overlapping. And the Bible promises you'll get much more than you give.

Poor old Grimm. His intentions were good. He didn't want to hurt anybody. And for sure, he didn't want to hurt himself. I think he learned a painful lesson. Hopefully you have too. At least the next time you're around a moving blender, don't lick it!

Chapter
Two

Chippie Doesn't Sing Much Anymore

A Texas newspaper reported the story. A Galveston housewife had a pet parakeet named Chippie. The woman made several mistakes. She was vacuuming her floors, and she decided to clean out the bottom of Chippie's cage with her vacuum cleaner. Mistake number one.

The phone rang. She turned to answer the phone without turning off the machine. You guessed it. Sssssssp! Chippie got sucked through the tube and into the canister. Mistake number two.

She dropped the phone, shut off the vacuum cleaner, and opened up the canister. There was Chippie—feathers askew, dirt all over his little body, stunned but alive. She rushed into the bathroom, bird in hand. She held Chippie under the faucet and turned it on full blast. Mistake number three.

Then she spotted the hair dryer. She turned it to "Hot" and "High." Mistake number four. The blast did the trick, but it nearly finished Chippie.

The next day the reporter called to check on the bird. "How's your poor parakeet?" the reporter inquired. It was about the reply you'd expect: "Well, Chippie doesn't sing much anymore. He just sort of sits there and stares."

I have the feeling many of you can relate to Chippie. You've had your cage vacuumed. You've felt sucked into the dirt bag, stuck under the faucet, and hit with a blast from a hair blower. And you don't sing much anymore. You just sort of sit there and stare.

We Were Born to Sing

I believe we were born to sing. Hank Williams sings the line, "I was born to boogie." I believe it's in the nature of all of us to be singers. Positive thinkers. Lots of people believe they were born naked. I believe you were born with a bright red ribbon wrapped around your body. On that ribbon were the words, "I am Lovable and Capable."

All babies believe this. They come to you with a wet diaper, runny nose, and drooling mouth. They can't believe that adults in their right minds could reject them. Babies believe they can do anything. It isn't just because they are immature and will learn better as they grow up. God Almighty intended them to have that ribbon. And the ribbon was meant to last a lifetime.

We keep that ribbon until we allow someone to take it away from us. Unfortunately we get a lot of help. But singing is normal. Believing is normal. God intended us all to be positive, loving, happy, and trusting.

The Song Stealers

There are lots of Chippie-style circumstances that steal our songs. Life sucks us all into the tube. People pour cold water on our dreams. Disappointment and disaster blow us away. Many people believe in Murphy's Law: What *can* go wrong *will* go wrong. Others believe in O'Toole's law: "Murphy was an optimist!"

Grief is defined in terms of loss, and life hands us a lot of losses. We can lose our jobs, our health, our money. We can lose our friends, our marriages, our self-esteem.

Life is full of accidents, diseases, and heartaches—the unexpected. There can be strong reversals. Cavett Robert says, "You can be *on Time* one week and be *doing time* the next!" There is no guarantee that life will be fair or that the sailing will be smooth. You're going to get blown off course. It's a foregone conclusion. It happens to us all.

There are a lot of song stealers out there. Some people seem to major in it. They'd rather let the wind out of your sails than inflate your ego. They're the ones who start out with, "Maybe I shouldn't tell you this, but . . ." There's not a chance they're not going to tell you. Gossips are afflicted with hoof-and-mouth disease. They're always hoofing it over to someone's house and mouthing off!

You can even steal your own song. There are those people who seem to be natural-born spreaders of gloom and doom—like the old lady who had "enjoyed poor health for twenty years."

I was on a plane with one of these folks. An elderly couple was seated in the row behind me. They were talking louder than they realized. "I don't like riding on these airplanes," the lady complained. "Folks get on them with guns and knives, and they take you places you don't want to go!"

> Gossips are afflicted with hoof-and-mouth disease. They're always hoofing it over to someone's house and mouthing off!

That got everyone's attention. The pilot and flight attendants were leaning out of the cockpit.

"Now, Honey," her frail little husband pleaded, "it's gonna be all right."

I smiled. You're always bumping into negative thinkers. I was busy with some work. We taxied to the end of the runway and burst up into the clouds. It was a beautiful day for flying. I didn't think about the little lady anymore until our wheels hit the runway at the next airport. At that precise moment her little old husband said optimistically, "You see, Honey, we made it all right."

And she shot back, "We ain't there yet!"

There are a lot of folks like that—the kind that can brighten up a whole room . . . just by leaving it! Someone said if you want to keep a positive attitude, you've got to stay away from the psychotics and the neurotics. There's a difference. The psychotic believes two and two are five. And if you hang around him long enough, I warn you, *you'll* end up believing two and two are five. But they don't affect you as much as the neurotic. He knows two and two are four . . . but it worries him.

Somewhere in the trauma of things, like Chippie, many people lose their songs. They just sort of sit there and stare.

How to Get Your Song Back

Has someone stolen your song? Have you forgotten how to sing? Here are five points on how to get your song back:

First, you've got to choose to sing. Some people choose to be croakers. Whiners. Complainers. Someone said, "Don't tell other people your problems. Eighty percent don't care, and the other 20 percent are kind of glad it happened to you." I don't know about that, but I do know we can all choose our attitudes.

I've studied aging. Some people become crotchety. Others have radiant dispositions. It's all a choice. No one can take away your song without your permission.

Second, you need to take singing lessons. Singing (positive radiance) is basically a gift, an art and a skill. It's something we can all learn. Isaac Traylor learned. When I was a little boy, our preacher, Roy Stephens, had a beautiful voice. One day Isaac said to him, "Roy, I'd give fifty dollars if I could sing like you."

I'll never forget Roy Stephens' reply, "Isaac, have you got fifty dollars?"

I don't know if any money exchanged hands. But I know that Roy taught, and Isaac Traylor studied, learned, and practiced with all his heart. He became a very good song leader.

But you've got to study *singers.* You can't hang around *croakers.* You'll become like the folks with whom you associate.

Third, you must think positive thoughts. Or in the case of singing, you must sing positive songs. "As [a man] thinketh in his heart, so is he" (Proverbs 23:7 KJV). Positive attitude teachers say, "Your life becomes what your mind is fed." Also, "It isn't what you think you are; it's what you think, you are!" The Bible says, "whatever is true, noble, right, pure, lovely, admirable, excellent, or praiseworthy, think about such things" (Philippians 4:8). When we realize we have power over what we think, we are on the road to getting our song back.

Fourth, you must get out of yourself. Someone said, "A man all wrapped up in himself makes a mighty small package." Selfishness robs us of our songs. People whose thoughts are turned inward cannot sing. They become selfish, self-centered, shallow, hollow, and silent. You must do something for others. "Do nothing out of selfish ambition or vain conceit, but

> You've got to study *singers.* You can't hang around *croakers.*

15

in humility consider others better than yourselves" (Philippians 2:3).

Fifth, fill your life with the Lord Jesus Christ. There is a beautiful story in the sixteenth chapter of Acts. Paul and Silas had been thrown into prison for preaching Christ. They had been attacked, beaten, and thrown into solitary confinement with their hands and feet fastened in stocks. Yet at midnight they were singing and praising God. Outward circumstances called for anything but singing. Crying, maybe. Fear and anxiety. Worry about what tomorrow would bring. But they were singing and praising God. Only a person whose life is filled with Jesus can do such a thing. They knew that even if they were killed, it would only vault them right into the presence of the Lord.

Our world is full of cage vacuumers, hair blowers, and song stealers. It's nice to know you don't have to just sit there and stare.

Open your mouth and sing this song by L. B. Bridges at the top of your voice,

> "Jesus, Jesus, Jesus,
> Sweetest name I know,
> Fills my every longing,
> Keeps me singing as I go."

Chapter Three

The Fine Art of Frog Kissing

You know the fairy tale, don't you? The wicked witch cast a spell on the handsome prince and turned him into a frog. He was doomed forever to that existence, unless a beautiful princess happened to come along and kiss him. Then the spell would be broken, he'd turn back into a prince, they would get married and, of course, live happily ever after. That's the way all fairy tales end.

Our daughter Tammy used to have a poster on her wall. It was a huge picture of a frog. The caption read, "To Find Your Prince Charming, You've Got to Kiss a Lot of Frogs!"

How would it feel to be a frog? Frogs are ugly, puffy animals, with warts all over them. They are slow and unattractive. They look "too pooped to pop." Did you ever feel like a frog? The frog feeling comes when you want to be the life of the party but come off as a clown. You want to contribute and cooperate, but you find yourself being selfish and introverted. You'd like to be big, but you feel so small. You're on the lily pad of life, drifting downstream, but you seem unable to shake the frog feeling. We need a beautiful maiden to come along, scoop us up, plant a passionate kiss on our lips, and transform us into everything we've ever wanted to be.

Everyone Feels Like a Frog Sometimes

I think there are times when all of us take on "frog mania." We feel like a klutz. We feel plain, not witty or clever. We say the wrong words and do the wrong things. We feel ugly, out of fashion, and we don't fit in. There we sit in our frog suits, while others talk about their world travels and exotic vacations. We recall that we once went to Iowa and watched the corn grow. It's like comparing the hustle and bustle of New York with going to my hometown's only intersection and watching the yellow light blink or going to town on Saturday to watch the barber cut hair.

I love that Charlie Brown cartoon—you know, the one where Charlie Brown, Lucy, and Schroeder are lying on the ground looking up at the clouds. Schroeder thinks he sees the likeness of Beethoven in the clouds, conducting his fifth symphony. Lucy sees George Washington, leading his men across the Delaware.

"And what do you see, Charlie Brown?" they ask.

Charlie Brown answers, "I was gonna say I saw a ducky and a horsey." Charlie felt like a frog.

It's easy to feel ordinary, intimidated, inferior, and stupid.

There's a Prince in All of Us

Do you believe in evolution? Well I *have* seen night owls on Saturday night turn into bed bugs on Sunday morning. Remember this poem?

Three Monkeys

Three monkeys sat in a coconut tree,
Discussing things as they're said to be.
Said one to another, Now listen you two,
There's a certain rumour that can't be true.
That man descends from our noble race.
Why the very idea is a disgrace!

No monkey ever deserted his wife,
Starved her baby and ruined her life.
And you've never known a mother monk,
To leave her babies with others to bunk.

Till they scarcely know who is their mother.
And another thing, my dear brother,
You'll never see
A monk build a fence around a coconut tree.
And let the coconuts go to waste,
Forbidding all other monks a taste.
Why, if I'd put a fence around this tree,
Starvation would force you to steal from me.

Here's another thing a monk won't do,
Go out at night and get on a stew.
Or use a gun or club or knife,
To take some other poor monkey's life.

Yes man descended, the ornery cuss,
But, brothers, he didn't descend from us!

Anonymous

Frogs come from tadpoles and are kissed into royalty! John was amazed at the transforming work of Christ. He said,

> How great is the love the Father has lavished on us, that we should be called children of God! And that is what we are! The reason the world does not know us is that it did not know him. Dear friends, now we are children of God, and what we will be has not yet been made known. But we know that when he appears, we shall be like him, for we shall see him as he is. (1 John 3:1–2)

God turned Saul the Persecutor into Paul the Proclaimer. He turned a plowboy, Elisha, into one of the greatest prophets in the Bible. He turned Samuel from a juvenile into a judge. And he worked his providence on David to make a kid into a king.

Only God could make a prince of the frog I see in the mirror every morning. I was uneducated, shy, and a low achiever, but a few people saw the prince in me and sought to help. God did his thing. Now this frog gets to preach in one of the greatest churches in America.

Only God could make a prince of the frog I see in the mirror every morning.

You know, we're always wanting to be someone else. Boy, oh boy, if I was only Kevin Costner. By the way, ladies, do you know what frustration is? It's when your husband and Kevin Costner fight over you, and your husband wins! But if I were Kevin Costner or Michael Jordan, I wouldn't get to preach for this great church. And although those two guys can do some things that I can't do, I can preach circles around either of them. Life's not too bad for this frog.

The Fine Art of Frog Kissing

And don't judge frogs too fast. I love Joel Hemphill's song:

He's Still Working on Me

There really ought to be
A sign upon my heart:
Don't judge him yet;
There's an unfinished part.
But I'll be better,
Just according to his plan,
Fashioned by the Master's loving hand.

He's still working on me,
To make me what I ought to be.
It took him just a week
To make the moon and stars,
The sun and earth and Jupiter and Mars.
How patient and loving he must be,
'Cause he's still working on me!

All most frogs need is a kiss. Kissing is plenty important. I have a news article with the headline, "Kissing Worth $275,000!"

It's the story of a lady who had an accident at her dentist's office. His drill slipped and broke. The resultant operation left her lower lip and jaw permanently numb. She claimed it caused a strain between her and her husband. She can't feel anything when he kisses her. They sued and won! The jury awarded the money. The only thing I can't figure out is why they gave the woman $260,000 and the husband only $15,000!

We have great potential. We just need the right one to touch us in the right way, and we'll be off and running on our white horses in no time at all.

Frog Kissing Is the Greatest Work in the World

Frog kissing is certainly the work of the church. Jesus calls our attention to the frogs of the world.

> When you give a luncheon or dinner, do not invite your friends, your brothers or relatives, or your rich neighbors; if you do, they may invite you back and so you will be repaid. But when you give a banquet, invite the poor, the crippled, the lame, the blind, and you will be blessed. (Luke 14:12)

Again,

> "Go to the street corners and invite to the banquet anyone you find." So the servants went out into the streets and gathered all the people they could find, both good and bad, and the wedding hall was filled with guests. (Matthew 22:9–10)

We look for princes when we want to build a church. We hunt up the ones with lots of money, influence, and talent. The church gets dignified. Sometimes we just get petrified. We unconsciously hang up our sign, "We Don't Want Any Frogs Around Here."

Frog kissing is certainly the work of the church.

Jesus was a frog kisser. "This man welcomes sinners and eats with them." Repugnant! Jesus hung around with a bunch of frogs. But he said, "It is not the healthy who need a doctor, but the sick" (Matthew 9:12). Jesus says look for the frogs. Once kissed, they'll become a mighty church.

Paul learned this when he preached in the ungodly city of Corinth. He spoke of frogs who had been "sexually immoral, idolaters, adulterers, male prostitutes, homosexual offenders, thieves, greedy, drunkards, slanderers and swindlers." Then came the classic statement, "And that is what some of you were. But you were washed, you were sanctified, you were justified in the name of the Lord Jesus Christ and by the Spirit of our God" (1 Corinthians 6:9–11).

Now that was a church full of frogs who had been kissed into princes and princesses. We've got to learn to see as Jesus sees: in every frog, he sees a prince. It's our business to kiss them with the Good News of Jesus and watch him change them into royalty!

Touch of the Master's Hand

Twas battered and scarred,
And the old auctioneer
Thought it scarcely worth his while
To waste much time on the old violin,
So he held it up with a smile.

What am I bid for the old violin?
Who'll start the bidding for me?
A dollar, a dollar, and who'll make it two?
Two dollars and who'll make it three?

Three dollars once, three dollars twice,
Going for three, but no!
From far in the back, a gray haired man,
Came forward and picked up the bow.

And wiping the dust from the old violin,
And tightening the loose strings.
He played a melody soft and sweet,
As a caroling angel sings!

The music ceased and the auctioneer,
With a voice that was soft and low,
Said, what am I bid for the old violin?
And he held it up with the bow!

A thousand dollars and who'll make it two?
Two thousand and who'll make it three?
Three thousand once, three thousand twice,
And going and gone said he!

The people cheered, but some of them cried,
We don't quite understand.
What changed its worth?
Swift came the reply,
The touch of the Master's hand!

And many a man with life out of tune,
And battered and scarred with sin
Is auctioned cheap to the thoughtless crowd,
Much like the old violin.

But the Master comes and the foolish crowd
Can never quite understand
The worth of a soul, and the change that's
    wrought
By the touch of the Master's hand!

Myra Brooks Welch

Turn It
Loose!

Remember that commercial where guys are shooting the rapids, grabbing life by the horns? It's real adventure and excitement. The song in the background chants, "Turn it loose!" You see it on T-shirts all over the place: "Turn it loose!" The guys on the river and that song—have a message for you and me!

There are so many people who never let themselves go. They never really live. They hold it all in. The song and those guys in the raft call to us. Grab life by the horns, they say. Throw caution to the wind. Really live!

Don't Turn Everything Loose

There are some things you should never turn loose. Undisciplined people will not be happy; they won't make others happy; they won't contribute much to the success of anything or anybody. Yet much of our music directs us that way. "I did it my way." "If loving you is wrong, I don't want to be right." "If it feels good do it; if it hurts leave it alone."

If you give a pig and a boy all they want, you'll have a good pig and a bad boy.

Unless you have some restraint, you'll be worthless to yourself and everyone else. I guess that's why God told Adam and Eve, "You can eat anything *except* that one tree." Guess which tree looked the best just then? Guess which fruit looked juiciest? Someone said if you give a pig and a boy all they want, you'll have a good pig and a bad boy. Unless you learn how to tell yourself (and others) *no,* you'll never really enjoy life.

Lots of things are better tied up: tempers, greed, lust, greed, the tongue. Ah, the tongue! The tongue is like a bit in a horse's mouth; it's like the rudder of a ship. And it's like the fire spark in a forest—it can never be tamed. It's full of deadly poison and set on fire by hell (see James 3).

But there are some things that need to be turned loose.

Turn Your Energy Loose

The word "enthusiasm" comes from the Greek words *en* and *theos,* which literally mean "full of God." There is boundless energy and enthusiasm in all of us. Are you tired? Too pooped to pop? Perhaps it's just mental weariness. Get moving! Energy is in there, probably just waiting to be jump started into life, waiting for a spark to ignite it into action. Housewives run marathons. Senior citizens climb mountains. You can do just about anything you make up your mind to do, but you've got to turn it loose. It's a mental decision.

Turn Your Laughter Loose

When was the last time you really cut loose and laughed? I mean a big belly laugh. Are you afraid your face might break? Do you hold back because of what someone else might think? They're probably hoping you'll go first and give *them* permission to laugh too. Laughter is good for you. The Bible says, "A happy heart makes the face cheerful" (Proverbs 15:13). "A cheerful heart is good medicine" (Proverbs 17:22). I'll bet you thought *Reader's Digest* coined the expression "Laughter is the best medicine."

Laughter is a valve. Remember blowing up balloons? After you blow the balloon up part way, you can stretch its neck, and it'll make a squealing noise as some of the air is let out. If you just keep on blowing air into the balloon, it will soon explode. Pieces of worthless balloon end up all over the floor. It's funny when it's just a balloon, but tragic when it's someone you love. Life is just like that. Stress builds up like air in a balloon, and laughter is just the release the doctor ordered. A good sense of humor is a must, if you want to live well and happy. So turn your laughter loose.

Turn Your Mind Loose

The human mind is so powerful. It's estimated that we use less than 10 percent of its potential. Just think—you can't overuse it, and you can't wear it out. It's there to help you explore, expand, and learn. Does the thought of getting older bother you? Do you worry about becoming senile? Here's a sure cure: never stop learning new things.

Don't lose your sense of wonder. Don't stop marveling at the beauty all around you. Don't be afraid to think new thoughts; write them down. Express your ideas; don't fear pursuing them. To get the best fruit, you've got to climb out on a limb. Turn it loose!

Turn Your Emotions Loose

Are you afraid to show your emotions? Is it hard for you to say "I love you," "I'm so proud of you," "I made a mistake," "Will you forgive me"? Were you brought up on "Big boys don't cry?"

"Jesus wept" (John 11:35). When his friend, Lazarus, died, even though Jesus knew he was going to raise Lazarus from the dead, he cried. Why did he cry? He cried because that's what people do when they lose someone they love. Thank you, Jesus. I needed that. How about you?

I'll tell you what to turn loose. Turn your anger loose, release your grudges, forgive those who've done you wrong. You say, "Yes, but they did it on purpose." Then forgive them on purpose. Stop blaming other people, stop blaming yourself, give your guilt to God, and accept his forgiveness.

Turn Your Money Loose

Say what? No, I'm not after your money. This is not a plea for you to send me your money with my promise of a fabulous return. But what I am saying is: become a giver. Someone noted the generous gift a rather prosperous man had given by saying, "I'd give, too, if I had what he has." But he probably has what he has *because* he gives like he gives.

Jesus said, "Give, and it will be given to you. A good measure, pressed down, shaken together and running over, will be poured into your lap. For with the measure you use, it will be measured to you" (Luke 6:38). And again, "It is more blessed to give than to receive" (Acts 20:35). The word *blessed* means *happy*. God wants you to be happy. So, turn your generosity loose.

Turn Your Music Loose

We are like different musical instruments in a marvelous orchestra. Each of us is designed to play in harmony with all the others. Together we become a magnificent symphony. If any piece is missing, if anyone cannot or will not play his part, something precious is lost. Your creativity, your individuality is needed for this world to make sense. You are so unique and valuable to the harmony of life. Please turn your music loose.

Turn Your Love Loose

Now I don't mean promiscuity or immorality. But God gave you the need and the capacity to love. You came with an owner's manual called the Holy Bible. It screams out, "Turn it loose!" "What the world needs now is love, sweet love." Don't hold such a treasure inside. Let it out. Be a lover. Don't be afraid to tell people you love them. Don't be afraid to show your love.

Start with your family. Let your spouse and kids know how much you love them. Expand your love to your relatives and close friends. Use those precious, golden words, "I love you," often and sincerely.

Get in the world's hugging line. Give and receive at least twelve hugs a day. You need at least four to survive, four more for maintenance, and four more for growth. Give hugs generously. Receive them gratefully.

Give pats on the back. Speak words of encouragement and affection. Drape your

Give hugs generously. Receive them gratefully.

33

face in a smile. It takes less effort to smile than frown: So give your face a break. Let others in on the good stuff. Give plenty of love, praise, and affection.

Love is a verb of action. God *"demonstrated* his love to us"* (Romans 5:6). Let's make sure we return the favor.

There's a rip-roaring, awe-inspiring life out there waiting for you. The challenge of the times calls for alertness, willingness, daringness, and optimism. So with an eye on God (the navigator) and his Word (the road map) and your hands firmly on the steering wheel, start your engines. Rev them up. Expect the best. And turn it loose!

Keep Your Cotton Pickin' Hands Off My Pickup Truck

I used to get a kick out of listening to Red Nekkerson on a local radio station. He was the typical rednecked, slow talking, backwoods bumpkin. One day he was talking about jealousy. Red's version went something like this:

> Some of you men are jealous. You don't want other men touching or hugging on your wives. You don't even want other men shaking hands with them. I'm just the opposite. My wife Nectarine and I love to go dancing. She likes all that hugging and touching. I ain't jealous. You can dance with my wife. You can hug her up. You can even give her a little kiss. But you'd better keep your cotton pickin' hands off my pickup truck!

I was in my favorite pickup truck when I heard Nekkerson. My good friend Gene Darby was with me. We laughed so hard we had to pull off the side of the road until we could gain control again. It was really funny. That is, it was funny until the other day.

Tuesday, April 2, I was coming out of the Casa Bonita Mexican restaurant in Tulsa. It was the day of our area preachers' lunch. The usual twenty-five or so preachers had been there doing all the stuff preachers like to do—a little eating, a little bragging, and a little politicking.

I headed for the parking lot, and my truck wasn't where I had left it. At first I thought I had just forgotten where I had parked it. But a thorough search of that parking lot revealed that my beloved pickup truck was gone. I mean *gone!* Somebody had stolen my truck within fifty feet of the front door of the restaurant while I was having lunch with a bunch of preachers. It was a beautiful sunny day, the truck was all locked up, and the keys were in my pocket. Gone!

I loved that truck. I could have easily tagged that day as "the day everything went wrong." I'd had an unexpected, long breakfast with a bunch of guys grappling with some frustrating problems. A staff meeting followed at the church, which lasted until lunch time. The preachers' lunch wasn't all that great either. As I recall, I got taken to task by someone there for some conviction I hold or some practice others wanted to criticize. It wasn't all that much fun. And then I went out to get in that beloved pickup truck. . . .

Perspective

And then *perspective* began to hit. The night before, our daughter had given birth to a brand new baby boy, presenting us with our first grandson. Momma was fine, baby was normal and healthy, and the father had . . . survived. God was still in heaven. I was still his child. I was standing there in good health. I had a ride waiting with one of the other ministers on my staff—a good friend and a great coworker. We were going back to a beautiful church complex to work for one of the finest churches in America. It was clearly a time for me to practice what I preach.

But This One Happened to Me!

Have you noticed that it's much easier to cope when it's someone else's problem? I can talk about *your* loss, *your* problem, and how to cope with it. I can give you advice; I can tell you what to do. I find it so easy to say, "If it were *me*, here's what I'd do." But this time it *was* me. That was *my* truck!

When it's your problem, your marriage, your health, your money, or your case they're on, it's a different matter. It isn't that logic and rationality won't work. I don't *want* it to work. I don't want advice; I want sympathy. I don't want advice; I *want my truck!* Only that day did I come to believe in capital punishment for truck rustlers.

Compared to What?

Remember the standard answer to the question, "How's your wife?" You say, "Compared to what?" Dr. Denis Waitley told of losing his beautiful California home in a terrible fire. His luxury cars were parked in the garage. Fire fighters were unable to get anything out. Everything went up in smoke: house, cars, furniture, clothes, and priceless, irreplaceable items. Totally lost! He said, "We've lost everything of value to us."

Then he realized he was standing there with his arm around his lovely wife. Their daughters, crying, were huddled close. And then it hit him. Everything that is *really* important was right there beside him. His wife and daughters were safe and healthy. Nothing was lost that was really important in comparison. "Besides," Denis chided, "all my income tax papers were lost in that fire, and I was due to be audited." He brought the house down with that statement.

I sat in the hospital room with a dear friend. He had previously had a leg amputated. But he was in the hospital today because his young wife was having a complete hysterectomy. He was really feeling low. I remembered a family I'd visited across the hall and said, "Come with me. There's someone I want you to meet." I took him across the hall where a small Mexican boy of about twelve lay in a coma. His head was narrow and extremely elongated, the result of an accident where a car tire actually ran over this young boy's head. My friend's eyes moved from the boy to the eyes of his terrified, grief-stricken parents. We went back across the hall.

The operation was a success. My friend's wife recovered nicely, and they went home to resume a rather normal, happy life. It's all "compared to what?" You see, I could move to Ethiopia. There are almost no truck thefts in Ethiopia. That's because there are almost no *trucks*. I think I'll just count my blessings and stay where I am.

What's the worst scenario you can paint? Is your marriage gone? Have you just been diagnosed with terminal cancer? Kids on drugs? Fired from your job? In the middle of a terrible lawsuit? It's still all "compared to what?"

God is still in heaven. He's still dealing in forgiveness, second chances, and mercy.

God is still in heaven. He's still dealing in forgiveness, second chances, and mercy. There is no sin that the blood of Jesus cannot cleanse. The Bible promises that "all things work together for good to them that love God" (Romans 8:28 KJV). God's family (the church) is still there. It's still an oasis in this desert of sorrow and sin. None of these temporary, earthly discomforts can change what's really important.

Don't Get Too Wrapped Up in Material Things

The song says, "Build your hopes on things eternal." But we still give far too much importance to fleeting things—trinkets and toys, status symbols, trucks and cars, furs and jewels, houses and furnishings. Often we chase *things* to the neglect of family, responsibility, and God.

> Do not store up for yourselves treasures on earth, where moth and rust destroy, and where thieves break in and steal. But store up for yourselves treasures in heaven, where moth and rust do not destroy, and where thieves do not break in and steal. For where your treasure is, there your heart will be also. (Matthew 6:19–21)

"It's great when you have things, but when *things* have you, it's bad."

America has lots of baubles and bangles. In pagan lands they bow to gods on totem poles and worship all kinds of statues, idols, and images. Americans wouldn't do that, would we? No, we'd just take on second jobs, live beyond our means, and sacrifice all peace and serenity just to possess a few more idols or status symbols or trucks. Someone said, "It's great when you have things, but when *things* have you, it's bad."

Life Goes On

I went to bed last night knowing this was the end. I could not face life without my truck. But the sun came up as usual this morning. I was able to get out of bed, slip on my running gear, and grind out four miles. It was a beautiful day. Spring was in the air. I got in my loaner car and drove to work. The day went just about the same as before. There were new problems but also new challenges. Nothing had really changed. And you know, the insurance company paid me for that stolen truck. Now I drive a brand new one, and I've nearly forgotten what that old thing looked like.

The Most Important Things Are Still Relationships

How do you feel about yourself? How is your relationship with your mate, your kids, and those wonderful grandkids? Do you have good close friends? Have you established and do you maintain a close relationship with God and his church family? If these relationships are close and real, you are rich, no matter what else you may not have. After all, these are the only things in life that really count. But if I ever catch that guy who stole my truck . . . !

Chapter Six

How to Get a Turtle on a Fence Post

Turtles do not climb fences. Turtles crawl on the ground, they swim in the water, but I'll bet you've never seen one climbing up the side of a fence post and sitting on the top! Yet Associated Press writer Anne S. Crowley, in an interview with renowned author Alex Haley, reports seeing a picture of a turtle perched right on the top of a fence post. Haley, author of the blockbuster book and movie, *Roots*, says, "Any time you see a turtle on top of a fence post, you know he had some help." It reminded Haley, and should remind us, that we don't get anywhere significant without help from others. Remembering this keeps us from singing our own praises.

Like the guy who titled his autobiography after the famous song *How Great Thou Art*, "A man singing his own praises is always off key." It reminds me of the story of the frog who developed the ingenious idea of going to Florida for the winter. He had two geese going that way to hold a stick in their beaks while he held onto it with his mouth. They were doing fine until passing over Tennessee when they were spotted by a couple of hillbillies below. One of them yelled, "Who came up with that great idea?" And the frog opened his big mouth and said, "I diiiiiiiiiiidddd!"

> "Any time you see a turtle on top of a fence post, you know he had some help."

Now you *can* get a turtle to sit on a fence post, but it's against his nature. It would certainly be an extraordinary accomplishment.

You'd have to . . . set your sights high; appropriate the right kind and amount of help; and just hang in there until the goal is reached.

Have you got any turtles you want to get on top of fence posts? Are there any goals in your life you really want to achieve, but like the chances of a turtle climbing a fence post, they seem out of the realm of possibility?

Just maybe we'll learn something from that turtle.

Accept Who You Are

Some parents tell their kids, "You're the best. You're better, smarter, prettier than all the other kids." And the poor kid fails trying to live up to your unrealistic expectations.

Why not tell them, "You're just like all the other kids in the world. You're not any better, but you're not any worse. We're all made out of the same old lump of clay." That means you can do what any other stumbling, fumbling, weak, inadequate human being has done.

Do you realize that's the only kind of people there are? Do you have trouble relating to the *greats* in the Bible or in the world around you? Listen to this verse: "Elijah was a man just like us. He prayed earnestly that it would not rain and it did not rain on the land for three and a half years. Again he prayed, and the heavens gave rain, and the earth produced its crops" (James 5:17–18).

Doctors, lawyers, scientists, teachers, inventors, preachers, athletes—they're all just like us. They just had different choices, motivation, and training.

The world's longest field goal (sixty-three yards) was kicked twenty-five years ago. It was the New Orleans Saints versus the Detroit Lions. The Saints were down 17–16. Billy Kilmer passed to the forty-yard line and called time out with two seconds left on the clock. They called Tom Dempsey onto the field, and the rest is history. The gun went off, ending the game, as the ball was in the air. It was good. The Saints won the game 19–17.

But the real story is that Tom Dempsey had one deformed hand and no toes on his kicking foot. In the aftergame interview reporters asked, "How does a handicapped guy kick a ball that far and that accurately?"

His reply? "I don't look on myself as handicapped. You can't worry about what you *don't* have. You've got to add up what you *do* have. You've got to bloom where you're planted!"

Appropriate Your Heritage

Many people live in Buts-ville or If-only-ville. "I could have done it, *but . . . if only* things had been different. . . . Please don't blame your alcoholic mother or your absentee father. Don't blame the system or the establishment. Learn that both bad and good upbringings can be used positively. An alcoholic father raises two children. One becomes a drunk and blames his parents; the other vows, "When I'm on my own, I'll do better than this." And he does.

We're thankful for the pilgrims who first settled America. We stand today on their shoulders. We are warming by fires we did not build. Others paid for freedoms we often take for granted. But many of those pilgrims were intolerant bigots. They had all kinds of prejudices, and scandal sprinkled their lives just as it does ours today.

I am blessed by my son's assessment of me. He says, "Dad, I believe you're one of the greatest men in the world, but I don't want to be just like you. I want all your good points, but I'm also studying others, and I want the best out of them too." That's good use of your heritage. Your past explains you, but it doesn't lock you in.

Get Help from Contemporary Successes

The key word here is "successes." Many people are busy copying others' flops just to prove they are orthodox.

You can't run with goats without smelling like them.

The rules for success are identifiable and learnable, and they are the same in any field. So study successes in business, marriage, relationships, morality, and spirituality.

Pick your friends carefully. You say, "My parents are always on me about my friends." Good! The Bible says, "Bad company corrupts good character" (1 Corinthians 15:33). You can't run with goats without smelling like them. And you can't fly with eagles if you hang around a bunch of turkeys.

Get Help from Education

Fortunately, in America we can be trained for just about anything. Educational opportunities are absolutely limitless. One man, who was enrolling his son in college, said, "It costs so much and takes so long to go through college. Isn't there a shorter course? Isn't there a cheaper way?" To his surprise the registrar replied, "Of course. It all depends on what you want to make of the boy." Cheaper and quicker is not always better.

Did you say you can't afford it? But can you afford to do without it? There's plenty of help available. If you are determined, you'll get it done. Hats off to those middle-aged and elderly people who are going back to school, taking night classes, and getting that GED.

Motivation Is the Key

Remember the plaque that reads, "I Could If I 'Vould,' but I Can't 'Vould' "? Motivation does wonderful things. I read of a woman watching her six-year-old playing in the surf. A small shark somehow got in the swimming area and clamped its jaws on the child's leg. The child was screaming for help. The frantic mother raced into the water, grappled her child with the shark still attached to its leg. She then proceeded to beat the shark to death on the beach. That's motivation.

We've all heard stories of someone picking up the back of a car to free a loved one trapped under it. And I love the story of the guy being chased by a bear. With the bear's hot breath on his back, he saw his only escape—a tree with a lone branch about fifteen feet off the ground. He leaped with all his might. Missed! But he caught it on the way down. Motivation!

I am privileged to appear professionally with some great motivational speakers in our nation. One of their common challenges is, "You can do anything you want to do. You can be anything you want to be. You can go anywhere you want to go. And you can have anything you want to have." How true!

The best book in the world on motivation is the Bible. Jesus says, "Everything is possible for him who believes" (Mark 9:23). Another powerful thought is, "What the mind of man can conceive and believe, his life can achieve."

The Best Help Is from Above

When the outlook is bad, try the uplook! Jesus said, "Ask and it will be given to you" (Matthew 7:7). Paul said, "I can do everything through him who gives me strength" (Philippians 4:13). And here's a warning: "You do not have, because you do not ask" (James 4:2). Believe in an active, powerful God. Develop a strong prayer life. Seek the help it takes. And believe in the outcome.

"What the mind of man can conceive and believe, his life can achieve."

Got any turtles you want up there? You can cry about turtles that have fallen off posts in the past. You can give reasons why your turtles never made it to the top. You can even ignore other people's turtles sitting up there pretty as you please. Or you can make up your mind to get some of your turtles up on fence posts. Do what it takes to get them there. Seek and appropriate the help you need. Commit the project to the good Lord, who can put anybody's turtle on any fence post . . . and keep him up there!

Never Wrestle with a Pig

Do you have a problem getting involved in needless quarreling? There are those who will argue at the drop of a hat. And *they'll* drop the hat. One guy said, "Pardon me for criticizing, but I have to do what I do best." We need to learn that we don't need to answer every question or deal with every issue. It's not necessary to respond to everything you disagree with. It's easy to get led into fussing and fighting, which results in stress, anguish, and hurt feelings.

I collect signs, placards, and posters with worthwhile ideas. One says,

> Never wrestle with a pig—
> you'll both get dirty,
> and the pig likes it!

People Will Try to Get You in the Mud

There are people in all areas of your life who will try to get you in the mud. Tragically some of these may be in your immediate family. Some spouses love to argue, gripe, whine, and generally turn heaven into hell. Sometimes it's a brother or sister. Or sometimes we hear, "My ex drives me crazy!"

You'll find mud wrestlers in the workplace, too. It can be your boss, your peers, even your subordinates. "They don't like me." "I'm being treated unfairly." "They have it in for me." And they're always mouthing off, looking for a fight. They can't stand peace and quiet. Watch out.

You'll find mud wrestlers in leadership. If politicians spent as much time and effort trying to help this country as they do wrestling with each other, most of our problems would be solved.

There are even mud wrestlers in the church. Some publications are just mud-wrestling journals, written by self-appointed "watchdogs," and "keepers of orthodoxy." Every issue is down on some issue or person. There are things we should stand against, but my goodness, tell me something you believe *in*. I guess some people just enjoy a good fight. They were born in the "objective case and kickative mood." They're not happy unless they're stirring up a stink. There is a *National Enquirer* syndrome among the Lord's people, and it's a crying shame! Try to answer them, and you end up in the mud with them. But remember, "you'll both get dirty, and the pig likes it!"

> Some people just enjoy a good fight. They were born in the "objective case and kickative mood."

How to Keep from Mud Wrestling

1. Keep smiling. It won't solve anything, but folks will wonder what you've been up to!

2. Live so you like yourself. Aside from God, you're the only one you have to please. Your face is the one you see in the glass. If you've pleased God, then you need to accept yourself.

3. Do your job as best you can. Just write down all the things you are: man, woman, husband, wife, father, mother. Do the same with your status and responsibilities at work, church, and in the community. Give it your best shot. And then don't jump in the mud with some pig.

4. Don't feel you have to compete with others. "We do not dare to classify ourselves or compare ourselves with some who commend themselves. When they measure themselves by themselves and compare themselves with themselves, they are not wise" (2 Corinthians 10:12).

5. Practice serenity. Choose to reject their rejection, to ignore their discourtesy. I learned a valuable lesson early in my preaching life. Someone had "written me up" in their local church bulletin. They said some rather unkind things about me and, frankly, lied about me. They had not come to me personally, and my name boldly graced their mud-wrestling editorial.

Well, it wasn't true. It wasn't fair, and I was going to get them at the next area preachers' luncheon. Trine Starnes, a fine, veteran gospel preacher was visiting our church in a gospel meeting. I took him with me to the neighboring town where the preachers' lunch was to be held. The editor of that article was to be there. I had him dead to rights, and I would take him to task right in front of all the other preachers. I was right, wasn't I? That was the way to handle it in a Christ-like manner, right?

Trine asked, "What will he do after you've had your say?" I admitted he'd probably be pretty upset. He would probably go after me again in his next bulletin article. Trine made me see it was a no-win situation. Then he delivered the knockout punch. He said, "Why don't you just put on a serene attitude? Greet him and all the others with charm and grace. That's all the vengeance you need, Marvin. And, you know, the Bible says, 'If your enemy is hungry, feed him; if he is thirsty, give him something to drink. In doing this, you will heap burning coals on his head'" (Romans 12:20).

I followed his advice. I had a wonderful lunch in sweet fellowship. The guilty preacher was the most miserable person there. I think he was just waiting for me to jump in the mud with him. I didn't satisfy his need and liking for mud wrestling.

6. *Give a soft answer to hard words.* "A gentle answer turns away wrath, but a harsh word stirs up anger" (Proverbs 15:1). Again, "Answer a fool according to his folly" (Proverbs 26:5).

I like this response to the one who has really cut you down with some unjust criticism. "Now that you've told me what's wrong with me, just to keep it in perspective, would you tell me one or two things you think I do well?" Ann Landers' answer to those who ask you unkind or personal questions is a classic. She says to look them straight in the eye and say, "Now why in the world would you ask a thing like that?"

7. *Ask yourself the classic question, "What does it matter?"* Paul was in jail. Some mud wrestlers sought to discredit Paul and make it seem as though it were his own fault that he was in prison. Sympathizers to Paul brought him the problem and wanted to know what to do about them. It wasn't right, and it wasn't fair! Paul's glorious answer was, "What does it matter? The important thing is that in every way, whether from false motives or true, Christ is preached. And because of this I rejoice" (Philippians 1:18). Keep those two priceless statements before you at all times: (1) What does it matter? (2) The important thing is . . . . That kind of thinking will keep you out of the mud.

What to Do about Criticism

It won't hurt you to listen when folks speak evil against you. Weigh carefully what is said. Introspect. Make an honest, personal evaluation. Pray. And then keep going in the direction you feel is right until you learn a better way.

Some people only want to stop you. Your critic owes you a positive solution to every negative criticism. If he can't produce that, he should just keep quiet. Don't respond to criticism; you can't please everyone. Pigs thrive on mud. They want you in there with them. Don't go! You'll both get dirty, and the pig likes it.

Keep about Your Work

The Lord has given to every man his work. It is his business to do it, and the devil's business to hinder him if he can. So sure as God has given you a work to do, Satan will try to hinder you. He may present other things more promising. He may allure you by worldly prospects; he may assault you with slander, torment you with false accusations, set you to work defending your character, employ pious persons to lie about you, editors to assail you, and excellent men to slander you. You may have Pilate and Herod, Annas and Caiphas all combine against you, and Judas standing by ready to sell you for thirty pieces of silver. You may wonder why all these things come upon you. Can you not see that the whole thing is brought about through the craft of the devil—to draw you off from your work and hinder your obedience to God?

Keep about your work. Do not flinch because the lion roars! Do not stop to stone the devil's dogs. Do not fool away your time chasing the devil's rabbits. Do your work! Let liars lie. Let sectarians quarrel. Let editors publish. Let the devil do his worst! But see to it that nothing hinders you from fulfilling the work that God has given you. He has not sent you to make money. He has not commanded you to get rich. He has never bidden you to defend your character, nor has he bidden you to contradict falsehoods about yourself which Satan and his servants may start to peddle. If you do these things, you will do nothing else. You will be at work for yourself and not for the Lord.

Keep about your work. Let your aim be as steady as a star. Let the world brawl and bubble. You may be assaulted, wrangled, insulted, slandered, wounded and rejected. You may be abused by foes, forsaken by friends, despised and rejected of men. But see to it with steadfast determination, with unfaltering zeal, that you pursue the great purpose of your life and the object of your being, until at last you can say, "I have finished the work which Thou gavest me to do!"

Author Unknown
Written over 90 years ago

I'm a motorcycle nut. Oh, it isn't that I get to ride all that much, but I own a full-size Honda Gold Wing. It's nine hundred pounds of black and chrome. I know the sights and sounds of that marvelous sport. I've done a few trips that topped a thousand miles. But most of my friends in the sport do that much every month. So it revved my engine, so to speak, when I read the news story about Hazel Kolb.

The headline read, "Motorcycling Grandma Ends Fifty-State Tour." It was 1987. Hazel Kolb was sixty-one, widowed, mother of four, and grandmother to seven. She had just driven her Harley Davidson up the steps of Juneau, Alaska, to complete visiting the capitols of the fifty states! The trip took three travel seasons (1985–87) and thirty thousand miles. This retired school bus driver has a stock reply for those who can't believe a feat like this. She says, "You just gotta get off your duff and go!"

I wrote to her. She sent me a copy of her latest book about her travels, and we exchanged a few letters. I did a *Peak of the Week* television program on her and sent her a cassette copy.

Hazel Kolb lost her husband in 1975. He owned a motorcycle, and they had enjoyed trips together around the nation. When he died she thought, "All those dreams and future plans are over." And then she began to realize, "There is nothing stopping me from taking that perimeter ride around the forty-eight states" she and her husband had always planned. All she needed was a motorcycle that was not too high off the ground. That's why she picked the Harley. And then she just got off her duff and went! She said, "I think all of us have goals, but we let them get on by. When the status of your life is such that you can do something, be it flying around the world or taking a sailboat across the ocean, then get off your duff and go!"

The sign on the back of her cycle reads, "Say hi to the motorcycling grandma." She began her tour in Tallahassee, Florida, on March 16, 1985. She finished the mainland. forty-eight states that year. Then she saved for the trip to Hawaii in '86. She rolled off the ferry in Juneau in '87 to complete the fifty states. Along the way she met ten governors. Her mission was to show that two-wheeling is a family sport. She wanted to get rid of the stigma that only bad guys ride cycles. She gives speeches at various rallies, but speaking or not, she is always inspirational with her gray hair, happy lines in her face, and positive words. She belongs to twelve motorcycle clubs and goes to as many rallies as she can afford. So she doesn't neglect those seven grandchildren, she often combines trips to rallies with visits to kids and grandkids. Perhaps there are some positive lessons we can learn from the motorcycling grandma.

Bloom Where You Are Planted

There are lots of "reasons" why Ms. Kolb should *not* be out there doing all that cycling. She's a woman, she's getting up there in years, and surely she gets lonely out there by herself. And there is always the possibility of an accident, danger on the roads, and mishaps of many kinds. But Hazel chooses to bloom where she's planted. She chooses this lifestyle over a pity party or a woe-is-me party.

If you're involved with any of the twelve-step programs, you'll sooner or later come across the Serenity Prayer. It goes like this:

> God grant me the serenity to accept
> the things I cannot change;
> Courage to change the things I can,
> and the wisdom to know the difference.

Attitude Is More Important Than Anything

Zig Ziglar says, "Attitude, more than aptitude, determines altitude." Attitude is just about everything. It isn't what happens to you, it's what you do about what happens to you that matters. Hazel Kolb is an active, smiling, get-with-it lady! The difference in her and any other person is really only attitude. It's an attitude that says, "I can live my own life, and I will do what I really want to do!"

The Importance of Setting Goals

"We aim at nothing; and then achieve it with remarkable accuracy" is a great statement. You've got to have goals. You can no more achieve anything worthwhile without them than you can come back from a place you haven't been. Remember what Hazel said: "We all have goals, but we let them get on by." So she set the goal to ride the perimeter states of America. Then she set a goal to write a book about her travels. Then she expanded her goals to visit all fifty state capitols on her cycle. Next she set a date for this, got off her duff, and hit the road.

There's no reason why any of us should not dream and reach out to claim our dreams. The worse thing about doing nothing is that you never know when you're through. We all have things we'd like to do. Make a plan, outline the goals, and set a date. Plan your life. Just do it!

Overcome Your Hindrances

There will always be hindrances to our dreams—reasons why we can't get them done. You can bet the sixty-one-year-old Motorcycle Grandma was surrounded by Negative Nellies. You know, they're the people who know all the reasons why you shouldn't be out there doing something silly like that. They conjure up all the bad things that might happen. Folks, the lights will never be all green. In the highway of life there will always be parts under construction. Bridges will be out. Detours, inclement weather, and unforeseen circumstances *will* be out there. If you wait for all the lights to be green at the same time, you'll never go anywhere. So, hey, be careful, but grab life by the horns and live it up! The blessings far outweigh the safety of a careful lifestyle! Some of these Negative Nellies get their exercise by *watching* an aerobics video.

> The worse thing about doing nothing is that you never know when you're through.

Anything Rewarding and Fulfilling Takes Time

But is it worth it? Ms. Kolb's husband died in 1975. She did the perimeter ride in 1979. She did the fifty states between 1985 and '87. Our trouble is we want it now. We won't attempt things that take much time. But you'll find that most things in life that are really worth doing take time—a lot of it. They take planning and money. I guess it just all depends on what kind of life you want to have. If excitement and adventure are in your blood, you'll listen to the lady who said "get off your duff and go!"

Last of all, Hazel Kolb says . . .

If you wait for all the lights to be green at the same time, you'll never go anywhere.

Accomplish and Then Keep Going

You see, this advice to "get off your duff and go" is an ongoing assignment. As soon as you finish one goal, set another. In the song, "Take Time to Be Holy," one line says, "Each victory will help you some other to win." Life should be one goal after another, one success followed by another, or one failure followed by another try.

I believe God invented life to be exciting, thrilling, and rewarding. It should bring peace, exhilaration, and success. The Christian life offers all these things, plus a fantastic eternity. If you're smart, you'll get off your duff and go!

A Closed Mouth Gathers No Feet

It was a strange visual aid the youth minister brought to class that night. "What's the most powerful weapon in the world?" he asked. The students named off the latest arsenal of weapons: airplanes, guns, bombs, explosives, nuclear missiles.

They were way off base, he said. He had the most powerful weapon right here in this little package. He had been to the butcher shop. And he unwrapped, right there in front of all those kids, a cow's tongue. Gross! "The tongue is the most powerful weapon in the world." And with that he read this from the book of James:

> When we put bits into the mouths of horses to make them obey us, we can turn the whole animal. Or take ships as an example. Although they

are so large and are driven by strong winds, they are steered by a very small rudder wherever the pilot wants to go. Likewise the tongue is a small part of the body, but it makes great boasts. Consider what a great forest is set on fire by a small spark. The tongue also is a fire, a world of evil among the parts of the body. It corrupts the whole person, sets the whole course of his life on fire, and is itself set on fire by hell. All kinds of animals, birds, reptiles and creatures of the sea are being tamed and have been tamed by man, but no man can tame the tongue. It is a restless evil, full of deadly poison. With the tongue we praise our Lord and Father, and with it we curse men, who have been made in God's likeness. Out of the same mouth come praise and cursing. My brothers, this should not be. (James 3:3–10)

These are harsh words! The tongue is a fire, a world of evil. It corrupts the whole person. Set on fire by hell, it cannot be tamed. It is a restless evil, full of deadly poison. Nothing gets us in more trouble than that little, wet, slippery creature that rests between our upper and lower teeth. You'd almost think we'd be better off without it, and maybe some people would.

Humans Alone Have This Marvelous Gift

Oh, I know animals have tongues. Animals make sounds, give signals, and emanate vibrations. Some have an uncanny ability to communicate. But humans alone can share, plan, discuss, and form conclusions. They can dream about their future, disagree, resolve, and strengthen relationships. Yet this phenomenal human ability is so unused, misused, and abused.

The Tongue Can Get You into a Lot of Trouble

"Don't put your tongue in motion before your mind is in gear." That's good advice, but we often talk, spilling out voluminous words, before we think it through. Here's another old saying I like: "He that talketh by the yard, but thinketh by the inch, should be kicketh by the foot."

An old, rich dying man said to his young wife, "When I die, I want you to get married again. You're young and beautiful and you have your whole life ahead of you."

"Nonsense!" she said.

"And I want you to give your next husband all my clothes. I want him to look good when he takes you out."

"Please don't talk that way," she said. "It's impossible."

"What's impossible about it?"

"You're a thirty-eight regular, and he's at least a forty-four long."

Did I say the tongue could get you into a heap of trouble?

The wrong tone of voice causes much of the friction in our daily lives. So don't give people a piece of your mind. You may have given too much of it away already!

> "He that talketh by the yard, but thinketh by the inch, should be kicketh by the foot."

Most of Our Problems Are Communication Problems

A married couple was sitting in their living room together. The husband sat next to an outside window. He said, as he looked out, "There goes that woman Harry is so crazy about."

His wife lunged for the window. She tripped over the carpet, broke a lamp, and nearly broke her neck. Then she said, "Idiot, that's Harry's *wife!*"

And he replied, "That's what I said."

Fred sat in a restaurant with a friend. He had just returned from an extensive trip to Africa. His friend asked, "Did anything unusual happen to you while you were over there in the jungle?"

"Not really!"

"Nothing unusual? No elephants, leopards, or warriors with poison darts?"

"No, but my buddy Ernie had an unusual experience!"

"Well, tell me about it," his friend said.

"I'll let him tell you about it himself." He took a small box from his shirt pocket and removed a little man, three inches tall. "Ernie, tell Frank here what you said that made that witch doctor so mad."

Communication!

Two men were struggling with a large crate in a doorway. They pushed and pulled until they were exhausted, but it would not move. One guy finally said, "It's no use. We're never going to get this thing in there!"

The other man replied, "*In* there? I thought we were trying to get it *out.*"

Good Advice on the Tongue

The Bible is replete with great information on how to use our marvelous tongues. Psalms and Proverbs are especially full of good advice. Here's a sample:

> Keep your tongue from evil and your lips from speaking lies. (Psalm 34:13)

> Reckless words pierce like a sword, but the tongue of the wise brings healing. (Proverbs 12:18)

A gentle answer turns away wrath, but a harsh word stirs up anger. The tongue of the wise commends knowledge, but the mouth of the fool gushes folly. . . . The tongue that brings healing is a tree of life, but a deceitful tongue crushes the spirit. (Proverbs 15:1–2, 4)

The tongue has the power of life and death. (Proverbs 18:21)

He who guards his mouth and his tongue keeps himself from calamity. (Proverbs 21:23)

Good Things from a Closed Mouth

We have a mouth, tongue, and voice box, and they can be used in wonderful ways. But sometimes it's best for a mouth to stay closed. We all need to become good listeners. Spouses, parents, preachers, elders, and friends really need to learn to listen. Most people don't need solutions; they just need someone to listen. Think of the thousands of psychologists, psychiatrists, and other therapists with overcrowded daily schedules. So many people feel the world has tuned them out. And they are willing to pay a hundred dollars an hour just to be heard. I'm not trying to minimize the great work of qualified practitioners, but many of them would be out of a job if there were an abundance of other good listeners around.

As the title of this chapter suggests, "A closed mouth gathers no feet!" Lots of people are possessed with foot-in-mouth disease, but you don't learn anything when you're doing all the talking. I have a friend who is a compulsive talker. She says, "You have to interrupt me at a comma; I don't ever come to a period." God gave us two ears and only one tongue. Maybe he intends for us to listen twice as much as we speak.

We've got to learn to listen without judging, learn to listen and ask questions. "Where will this lead?" "If you do this, will you regret it later?"

Listening keeps you from misjudging a situation. "Digging for facts is a lot better exercise than jumping to conclusions." But that's the only exercise some people get. "He who answers before listening—that is his folly and his shame" (Proverbs 18:13).

> "Digging for facts is a lot better exercise than jumping to conclusions."

Listening also keeps you from the dangerous sin of gossip. Here's a saying I like about gossip: "If the gossiper should be hanged by the tongue, then the one who listens to gossip should be hanged by the ears."

Listening also keeps you from quarreling. Here are some other sins you can avoid by keeping your mouth closed: lying, slander, dirty stories, cursing, and negative talk.

Don't judge others' motives. Don't always have to insert your opinion. Sometimes, just listen.

Good Things from an Open Mouth

God gave you a mouth to use. When your mouth opens, let it say sweet stuff. Talk of good things—things that are beautiful, right, just, and merciful. Let it compliment and encourage other people. Let it teach goodness, manners, and patience. Let it tell the Good News about Jesus and confess his holy name. Let the tongue express love, affection, and reassurance. Let it apologize sincerely. Let it praise God from whom all blessings flow. Let it express thanks for nature, good friends, and family. Let it forgive "seventy times seven."

So open your mouth to speak about what is good. And above all remember that "a closed mouth gathers no feet!"

Like Paul Harvey, I like bumper stickers. He hunts "bumper snickers" and reads them on his radio show. Someone sent him one they had seen in the Philippines. It read, "Yankee Go Home." In smaller letters it said, "and take me with you!"

One study tried to find the best place in the world to live. It considered cost of living, wages and job opportunities, housing, and child-rearing environment. And guess what? You live right in the middle of it, if you live in the good old United States of America. With all of America's problems, and she has several, this is still the best place in the world to live.

But back to bumper stickers. I saw one the other day that read, "This Is Not a Bumper Sticker!" A plumber's van wore one that advertised, "In Our Business a Flush Beats a Full House." I'd agree with that one.

Here are some others that have caught my eye. "I May Be Slow But I'm Ahead of You"—usually seen on the bumper of a clunker. How about, "If You're Rich, I'm Single." Then there's another for an old, outdated car: "Yes, But It's Paid For."

I had to laugh at "Ex-Husband in Trunk." That bit of humor probably covered a multitude of bitterness and anxiety.

A few years ago a well-known church came up with "I Found It!" It had a nice message about finding the Good News about Jesus. But someone else blew it with this bumper sticker answer: "I Lost It!"

But the one that caught my eye is the subject of this chapter: "Don't Follow Me, I'm Lost!" It reminds me of the story Jesus told in Matthew 15:1–14. The Pharisees and teachers of the Law should have been the leading religious people of the day. If anyone knew God, they should have. If anyone practiced caring and loving religion, it should have been them. But they were so hypocritical. Their religion was so shallow and legalistic. They were all form and no substance. Jesus called them clouds without rain. He called them whitewashed tombs—pretty on the outside, but full of dead men's bones. He said, "These people honor me with their lips, but their hearts are far from me. They worship me in vain." Then came the most serious indictment: "Leave them alone. They are blind guides. If a blind man leads a blind man, both will fall into a pit."

These lost leaders were more interested in ritual than righteousness. They were more wrapped up in hand washing than in soul washing. They criticized Jesus' disciples when their own lives were full of dishonor and shame. Jesus called them blind guides. To follow them would be to fall into the ditch with them. You've got to watch who you follow.

Bumper Stickers Can Be Seriously Wrong

Bumper-sticker "pulpits" scream out a lot of things that can get you in a heap of trouble. There is so much wrong and warped thinking that seeps into our minds from bumpers—and from television programs, movies, books, and magazines. Here are a few:

- "If it feels good, do it; if it hurts leave it alone."
- "Break any rule if you can make a quick buck."
- "Get to the top no matter who you have to walk on."
- "If you love him, leave your marriage, family, kids, and anything else that stands in the way of your happiness."
- "Everybody's doing it."
- "Just once won't hurt."
- "You're only young once."

And there are lots of bad examples around. Lots of poor kids *without* see drug pushers *with!* They've got lots of money, wear sharp clothes, and drive fine automobiles. It teaches this misleading lesson: violate the law, walk on the rights of others, and you'll go to the top. You'll have plenty of everything that makes for success. But there are very few *old* drug dealers. They're either caught and sent to prison, or they die in some horrible way while still in their prime.

Couple this with the same kids' chances of becoming doctors, sports superstars, preachers, or anything else decent and successful. It reminds me of a tombstone on which was inscribed,

> As you are now, so once was I.
> Be warned, my friend, you too will die.
> As I am now, soon you will be.

Prepare, my friend, to follow me.

And someone had scrawled underneath,

To follow you I'm not content,
Until I know which way you went.

Everybody Follows Somebody

Years ago Bob Dylan came out with the song, "You Gotta Serve Somebody." The Bible says, "You are slaves to the one whom you obey—whether you are slaves to sin, which leads to death, or to obedience which leads to right-eousness" (Romans 6:16). Lots of things compete to enslave us.

There are many ways to see whose slave you are. Your check stubs indicate how you spend your money. They show what's important to you. Your appointment calendar is another indicator. You only have so much time. Every thing scheduled means something else cannot be scheduled. The things you give priority to indicate what is important to you. Other indicators are the people you choose to hang around and the causes you support. All these things spell out whose servant you are.

I'm reminded of a guy I saw walking down the street with those sandwich advertising boards hanging on his body. On the front, his sign read, "I'm a fool for Christ" (1 Corinthians 4:10). On the back, it read, "Whose fool are you?" Pretty impactive.

Many voices call us to follow. Fashion is one. Are you surprised? That label on the hip pocket of your jeans is a mighty powerful master to a lot of people. Calvin Klein. Oscar de la Renta. Jordache. Guess. But a housebrand of a local discount store? Many people wouldn't be caught dead without a recognized name on their jeans, shoes, or shirts.

Popularity is another strong voice that calls us to follow. The Bible mentions that many of the religious leaders believed in Jesus but would not confess him openly "for they loved praise from men more than praise from God" (John 12:43). Peer pressure. Many go along with things they don't believe in and don't feel good about. They are afraid to stand against the crowd. So they compromise their morals, their integrity, and their faith. They offer what they know is right on the altar of popularity.

Pleasure is a strong voice. But the apostle Paul said, "If I were still trying to please men, I would not be a servant of Christ" (Galatians 1:10). Other voices are sex, power, and materialism. The ones we listen to identify whose servants we are.

But God also calls: "Come to me, all you who are weary and burdened, and I will give you rest. Take my yoke upon you and learn from me, for I am gentle and humble in heart, and you will find rest for your souls. For my yoke is easy and my burden is light" (Matthew 11:28–30).

Where You Go Is Determined by Who You Follow

That's why Jesus said, "If the blind lead the blind, both fall in the ditch." Too many Christians pattern their lives after the wrong people. Many celebrities have lost their sense of responsibility. They ignore the millions who follow their example. They say, "What I do is my business," and "I'm not responsible for what someone else does." But watch those fans "ape" their heroes. They dress like their heroes dress, drink like they drink, and abandon morals and ethics just as they see their idols do. America is paying the price of "following the blind." That price is broken marriages, kids overdosing on drugs, a skyrocketing suicide rate among the young, and a nation with its back turned on God. J. Paul Getty, the oil billionaire, once said, "I'd give all the money I own for the love of a good woman." He could have had it too, but he was following the wrong bumper sticker. How about you?

Marching to a Different Drummer!

Henry David Thoreau and Ralph Waldo Emerson were great friends. Thoreau was known for his strong convictions, even if they were not always popular. He refused to pay a certain tax because he felt it was unjust. As a result he was thrown into jail. Emerson heard his friend was in jail and rushed over to see him.

"Henry," he said, "what in the world are you doing in there?"

Thoreau replied, "Nay, Ralph, the question is, 'What are you doing out there?'"

If you don't stand for something, you'll fall for anything.

You see, if you don't *stand* for something, you'll *fall* for anything. The Bible says, "Bad company corrupts good character" (1 Corinthians 15:33). They say silence is golden, but sometimes it's just plain yellow.

There are plenty of good role models out there to follow—plenty of people who are not lost. They know who they are, whose they are, what they are doing, and where they are going.

Jesus' bumper sticker reads, "Follow Me—I Know the Father." "Follow Me—I'm Going Home." So with all these confusing bumper stickers around, don't get lost in the traffic.

If You Want to Run with the Big Dogs, You've Got to Get Off the Porch

Ben and Pearl Traylor are our closest friends. We often take trips together. One time we were in Eureka Springs, Arkansas—a hillbilly town with lots of arts and crafts shops. While our wives shopped for other things, Ben and I got our laughs reading baseball caps.

One cap said, "This is my gun-jamming, dog-losing, deer-missing hunting cap." You've probably seen the one with the two bills that says, "Which way did they go? I'm their leader!" Another one said, "Ex-wife for sale; take over alimony payments." We got a big laugh out of the one that said, "My wife ran off with my best friend . . . and I sure do miss *him*."

And then there was this one: "If You Want to Run with the Big Dogs, You've Got to Get Off the Porch." That one's up my alley. It talks about the motivation it takes to get to the top, to fulfill your dreams, and to reach your goals.

That Special Three Percent

A lot of people go to positive-thinking rallies and special seminars on how to set and reach incredible goals. I've spoken at a few of these with guys like Zig Ziglar, Cavett Robert, Dr. Norman Vincent Peale, Paul Harvey, and Art Linkletter. Thousands were in the audience. They all made the decision to come, spent their money, and took time off from work. Sometimes they arranged to travel many miles and stay overnight just to attend that seminar.

The speakers were good. They told us how to set and reach our goals. They shared their own stories and were living proof that it could be done.

But, you know, most people *don't* make it. They all *want* to make more money; they *want* more success. They sit spellbound, take notes, buy tapes and books. But when they get back home, they are mostly the same people they were before they came. They *want* a greater measure of success, but it eludes them. Why?

Only about 3 percent of a given audience will, in fact, put the principles into action. Only 3 percent will deliberately make a choice, pay the price (my good friend Zig Ziglar says, "enjoy the price"), and achieve the goal. Others want to, but they never do anything about it. Alcoholics say there are two kinds of drinkers: those who want to quit, and those who *wish* they wanted to quit.

The 3 percent show dramatic life changes. They grab a greater measure of success than all the others. It isn't that others could not do it. It isn't that IQ, sex, age, or race exclude certain people from the winners' circle. It isn't that there's no more room at the top. It's because most people won't leave their *comfort zone*. They won't leave the porch. They'll never run with the big dogs.

Life Is Easier on the Porch

You can get by on the porch. The porch is safe. It poses few threats, but it offers little joy. The porch is the place of compromise. There are lots of average people out there, and they compliment themselves on being average. "I'm just an average sort of guy," they say. Listen to Paul Harvey's definition of average: "If you're average, then you're the best of the lousiest and the lousiest of the best." Ouch!

Two guys were pushing a heavy cart up a steep hill. They finally made it to the top.

"Man," the first guy said, "I thought we'd never make it. I thought any minute the thing would stop and roll back down the hill."

The other replied, "I thought so too. So I kept the brake on all the way up."

Guess which one was the big dog.

Rivers are beautiful, especially when seen from the air. I like flying in small airplanes—you're closer to the ground, and the view is spectacular. You can make out horses and cattle in the fields. A friend of mine told how he used to fly his helicopter low over a farmer's field. He'd spot a watermelon patch, make a brief landing, and fly off with a choice melon. I'm not telling you his name, but there were buckshots in the sides of his helicopter.

Anyway, one day a friend was flying me to a speaking engagement in his private plane. It was a beautiful day. The sun bathed the earth with its golden light and splashed a silver ribbon across a lovely, winding river. Now that's beauty. But the beauty suddenly disappeared when I asked myself, "Where is that river going?" I knew the answer in a hurry. It's going slowly, aimlessly, *down*. That's okay for rivers, but not for people.

The porch is a place of mediocrity for mediocre people, mediocre marriages, mediocre businesses, and mediocre churches. You may feel less like a failure on the porch, but the big dogs, and the big people, are out there running all over the place—accomplishing and innovating. They are right in the middle of what's going on.

Fear is what keeps people on the porch. They're fenced in by their comfort zone. Do you know why folks are afraid to take risks? Because risks are *risky!* They demand that you do something you've never done before, and they offer no guarantees for success. Porch dwellers dwell on all the negative possibilities. They want *something* for *nothing*, but nothing is all they'll get on the porch.

True, the porch poses no risks, but it also offers no reward. Those are the conditions you live by if you stay on the porch.

Porch Dogs

Some dogs just seem made for the porch. They are content to let other dogs meet the challenges and chase the dreams. They bark but never chase. They open one eye as excitement and adventure run by, but all they do is look. Porch dogs offer no protection, don't have to be pretty, and don't cost much money. You can get this kind of dog at the pound or find them abandoned at the city dump. You can buy them for a few dollars. But I warn you, you get what you pay for.

Now there are big dogs galore—you know the kind: show dogs, hunting dogs, breeding dogs, seeing-eye dogs, and dogs trained to be in the K-9 corps. Some have been taken off the porch or out of an alley. They've been groomed, fed, and trained for excellence. These dogs have been disciplined through rugged competition and now wear championship ribbons around their necks. They bring top dollar at dog shows and get to live a champion's lifestyle. That's the difference in dogs

Risks demand that you do something you've never done before, and they offer no guarantees for success.

who lie on the porch and dream and those who get off the porch and run!

Success Is for Those Who Get Off the Porch

Three laws govern sowing and reaping—not just theories or possibilities, but *laws:*

> You will reap *what* you sow.
> You will reap *more* than you sow.
> You will reap *later* than you sow.

Anyone can test this. It works in farming. Plant corn, and you'll get corn—nothing else. And that one kernel of corn doesn't produce a stalk with a single grain of corn on the end; it shoots toward the sky, and dozens of ears of corn appear, each with row after row of corn. It also takes time. Our problem in America is that we want to throw the egg in the henhouse at night and hear it crow in the morning. Like the sign on the highway that read, "Antiques Manufactured—While You Wait."

If you plant the right stuff and nurture it properly, before long a bumper crop will be yours. That's the story of life. There's plenty of opportunity out there for us all. The Bible says, "Do not be deceived: God cannot be mocked. A man reaps what he sows" (Galatians 6:7).

Another marvelous truth is this:

> You can get anything in life you want, if you just help enough other people get what they want.

There are so many worthwhile goals, such as a great marriage, a thriving business career, and a dynamic church. We need health goals, financial goals, and educational goals. And most important, we need great spiritual goals. But you can't watch it all happen from the porch. Remember the saying, "Everything comes to him who waits"? In this case, waiting yields mediocrity and failure. Get off the porch—today!

The Difference between Porch Dogs and Champions Is Minimal

One horse wins the Kentucky Derby. His owner is paid thousands of dollars. He and the jockey stand in the winner's circle. A wreath of flowers is around that horse's neck, and it's picture is in the paper. Horse breeders pay top stud fees to have a colt from that horse.

Now take a look at the horse that places fourth. The money is hardly mentionable. Why? Because the winning horse was four times faster, right? Wrong! They finished with only a fraction of a second difference in time.

Remember that 3 percent? The batter stands at the plate. He swings and you can hear the crack of the bat. Every eye follows the ball to the fence. The left fielder is on the run. At the last minute he leaps into the air, glove extended to the max. The difference between a grand slam homer and the third out is only three inches! You can be in a telephone booth with twenty-four cents, and you can't even reach the operator.

> The difference between "try" and "triumph" is just a little "umph!"

You see, the difference between a porch dog and a big dog is just a little motivation. The difference between success and failure is often something very small. A friend of mine who's an elected official asked me to write a speech for him. I called it "Don't Just Try . . . Triumph." You see the difference between "try" and "triumph" is just a little "umph!" The journey of a thousand miles begins with a single step. And you'll never go very far on the road of success as long as you keep one foot on the porch. Even turtles know that in order to get anywhere they have to stick their necks out.

Now you can play it safe with 97 percent of the dogs. Or you can grab life and opportunity by the horns and go for it. The difference is whether or not you are willing to get off the porch!

Chapter Twelve

They've Just Slapped My Other Cheek

It was the mother of all bad luck days. For Brian Heise, Brigham Young University Students' day was one calamity after another. He kept wondering if God wanted him dead but just kept missing. It was the fourth of July, and it was raining. He was to be in a parade that day. Raining! He heard the sounds. Wait a minute. The sounds were coming from *inside* the house.

A water pipe in a neighbor's apartment right over Brian's had ruptured. Water poured from the walls and electrical outlets in Brian's apartment. He ran to his car to go rent a water vac. But his car had a flat tire. He changed the tire, then went back inside to call a friend to come help with the cleanup. As he picked up the phone, he was zapped by an electrical shock. When he jumped back, the phone fell off the wall.

Brian decided to go back out to his car, but the water had swelled the front door shut, and he couldn't get outside. He finally kicked the door open only to find that his car had been stolen. Because there was little gas in his car, he knew the thief wouldn't get far. He found the car a few blocks away and pushed it to a service station. He bought gas, rented the vacuum, and returned to clean up his apartment.

Heise, a member of a Civil War nostalgia group, got into his Civil War uniform for the parade and walked outside. But he found a parade float blocking his driveway. So he missed the parade. But never mind, there was to be a mock battle at the Brigham Young University football stadium later that evening. He'd get in on that.

That evening he participated without incident in the battle. But as he returned to his seat, he sat on his bayonet, which sank into his backside several inches. Because of the traffic jam, Heise had to walk to a local clinic where a doctor fixed him up. A friend gave him a ride home, but when he got there, he slipped on the wet carpet and badly bruised his tailbone. "They say turn the other cheek," he said, "but I only have one left to sit on."

We Can All Relate to Stress

Stress is the number one killer in America. It's responsible for strokes, heart attacks, high blood pressure, migraines, colitis, and a hundred other things. It's behind most, if not all, the ills that track us today. Stress has been defined as "that confusion created when one's mind overrides the body's desire to choke the living daylights out of a jerk who desperately needs it." (Admittedly, this is not a Billy Graham definition.)

It's been one of those weeks. You know the feeling don't you? You're facing time deadlines, unrealistic expectations, people problems, and a stack of calls to return. The report from the doctor was not good, and the estimate to fix the roof was several hundred dollars more than you had anticipated. You have piles of bills to pay. The car is broken down. Your ex is giving you a hassle over child support and alimony. The kids are screaming, and your new marriage is in trouble. And on top of all that, your ballpoint pen is leaking!

I Know about Other Cheeks

I go to church and read the Bible, so I know all the verses. Turn the other cheek. If someone strikes you on one cheek, turn the other also. Go the second mile. Return good for evil. "If your enemy is hungry, feed him; if he is thirsty give him something to drink. In doing this, you will heap burning coals on his head" (Romans 12:20). (I like that one.)

It reminds me of the couple counseling with their minister about their marriage. The preacher asked, "Well, Maggie, have you tried heaping coals of fire on his head?"

"No, but I poured boiling water down his leg!" Oops!

I believe those verses. They are right, and they work. I just want to know how to do it. Why are they so hard to do? Where is the motivation to live that way?

I've heard all the arguments. Respond, don't react. Do unto others as you would have them do to you. Let a smile be your umbrella. (Well I did once, and I got beastly wet!) This is one I love: Cheer up; things could get worse. (So *I* did, and *they* did!)

I'm like the two mosquitoes who were flying over the nudist camp. One said, "I know what I'm supposed to do. I just don't know where to start." I know I'm supposed to love my enemy, but today I think he's a jerk. He desperately needs my hands on his throat till the life is squeezed out of his miserable little body.

Stress Fractures

All athletes know about stress fractures. They are tiny microscopic cracks in the outer layers of bone. They are caused from all that shock and strain of the constant pounding and straining that an athlete's body gets. Stress fractures are usually found in the legs and feet. They often go unnoticed, but if the pounding continues, the cracks aren't allowed to heal. So, they enlarge and cause excruciating pain. They force you out of the game and maybe out of sports altogether.

On November 7, 1986, Sam Bowie—big, tall center of the Portland Trailblazers—went up for a jump shot. People sitting in the stands were close enough to hear the "crack." He landed in shooting pain, with his shinbone almost protruding out of his leg. Sam's hidden stress fracture had suddenly become public knowledge. That microscopic crack had exploded into a compound fracture that threatened to end his career.

Stress fractures are not limited to athletes, nor even to the physical body. Tiny cracks in the bone are nothing compared to the cracks that wrench our hearts. Your spirit can be suffering from stress fractures. It's what we mean by a broken or aching heart. There's real pain there that hangs on, deep and haunting. The pain won't go away. It seizes your chest in a tightness that you can't escape in the early predawn hours.

Some people treat their pain with alcohol, drugs, or extramarital affairs. They increase the tempo of their already overcrowded schedules. It's like pouring gasoline on a fire.

What Are We to Do?

Physically, we've got to "give it a rest." Jogging is an interesting sport. It incurs all kinds of running injuries. Besides stress fractures, there are tendinitis, shin splints, and stitches. Some runners try to "run through" them. They figure if they just stay out there and don't give in, the problems will somehow go away. This is a good way to compound the injury. Many joggers have had to give up running altogether because they "ran through" the injury. Rest is the only cure.

We've got to stop the pounding. Some people are just too intense. Lighten up. Laugh more. Admit your imperfections. Let some stuff go. Don't try to be Superman, Batman, and Rambo all combined. Stop to talk to a child or visit an elderly person in a nursing home. Get away for a purely fun weekend. Go see a good movie. Curl up by a crackling fire with a good book. Lay outside at night and gaze up at the stars. Cancel appointments that are not really all that important.

Prayer helps. God has no problem hearing our hurts. He's our Father, and fathers love their kids and want the best for them. He can keep secrets too.

Throw away any letter that sharply criticizes you. Don't answer hate mail. That's the only good in anonymous letters—you can't answer them. Read your Bible. Visit a friend who can't get out of the house. Commit, and then recommit your life to Christ.

Does all this sound irresponsible? Well, it works! And it's a whole lot better than choking the liver out of some jerk and winding up in the clink.

Lighten up. Laugh more. Don't try to be Superman, Batman, and Rambo all combined.

Keep Your Head in the Game!

A few years ago the New York Mets faced the Atlanta Braves. With two outs, Atlanta had runners on first and third. Dave Cone was on the mound for the Mets, and Mark Lemke stood at the plate for the Braves. Lemke hit a ground ball between first and second. Cone, as pitchers are supposed to do, ran to cover first. It was a close call: "Safe!" The umpire said Cone failed to touch the bag.

Cone flew into a rage. He got in the face of umpire Charlie Williams. He protested. He screamed! He kicked dust into the air. And all this time Dave Cone had the ball clutched firmly in his hand. One of his teammates grabbed him from behind. He tried to get the ball. But Cone held on to it tenaciously, not even realizing it was in his hand. His teammate yelled for him to "get your head back in the game."

In the meantime, with Cone's back to the infield, the runners who had been on first and second scored. The Mets lost the game because of it. Dave Cone, embarrassed, later admitted his mistake. "I snapped," he said. "It cost us the game. It's all my fault."

Before We Criticize Dave Cone . . .

Maybe we'd better take a serious, personal inventory. Have you let an angry blowup over some petty incident destroy a friendship that took years to build? Have you let one out-of-character mistake cost you a marriage that had lasted more than twenty years? One of the most well-known and loved Christian ministers and authors was involved in an affair at the time he was writing his best-selling book. When someone asked his wife why she stood beside her husband when he had done her so wrong, she said, "That was just one mistake in a lifetime of love and loyalty." I think her head was in the game.

Parents, do you let yourselves get preoccupied with getting ahead and keeping up with the Joneses and then blow it in parenting your children? You can yell and scream, uncharacteristically, over some petty issue and watch a relationship go out the window.

Churches get sidetracked so easily. We can focus on petty internal issues, while a whole world goes to hell. The larger picture is lost while we argue over the color of the carpet or who stole a roll of paper towels from the rest room.

> Churches get sidetracked so easily. We can focus on petty internal issues, while a whole world goes to hell.

We Don't Have Eyes in the Backs of Our Heads

That was Dave Cone's problem. His eyes were blazing at the umpire who called that runner safe. So he could not see behind him as two runners scored and won the game. When we totally focus on one thing, we're blind to the things outside our peripheral vision. When we choose to concentrate on one thing, other things go unnoticed and unattended.

A man wrote about attending the funeral of the beloved King George VI of England. The royalty of the world was in attendance. Thousands lined the streets to see this grand procession and to catch a glimpse of the cart that carried the beloved king's body.

King George had a little dog named Caesar. As the parade passed ceremoniously down the street, Caesar trotted along under the wagon carrying the casket. As the parade drew near, a cur dog ran out of the crowd, barking at Caesar. The man wrote, "As I turned to watch that dog fight, five kings passed by!" I think we may add that as we turn our attention to trivials, the important things of life go by unattended. As we devote our energies and devotion to lesser things, Jesus Christ, King of Kings, Lord of Lords, passes by unnoticed.

We Must Focus on the Right Things

It doesn't mean that we are bad people. We simply can't do it all or have it all. Every decision that *includes* also *excludes*. Back in the depression days, before paved roads, there was a roadsign that read,

Choose Your Ruts Carefully;
You'll Be in Them for the Next Twenty Miles!

One decision allows you to really give time, attention, and energy to a given project. But that same decision locks you out of whatever else could have been done in that time frame. It's a frightening lesson in priorities. How easy it is to allow the incidental to take precedence over the important. The menial defeats the meaningful. The temporary reigns at the expense of the permanent.

The apostle Paul writes, "So we fix our eyes not on what is seen, but on what is unseen. For what is seen is temporary, but what is unseen is eternal." (2 Corinthians 4:18).

What Is Really Important?

Dave Cone missed it that day. He was so sure he had his foot on the bag that he felt he *must* argue his case. And he did so at the cost of the game. He was so distracted by this personal "injustice" that he missed the fact that runners, behind his back, were scoring the winning runs.

One Sunday afternoon in Rome, visiting day in the local jail, some admirers of the grand old apostle Paul came to visit their incarcerated friend. They were agitated and related to Paul that some young whippersnapper had been in the pulpit that morning. He had spouted that it was Paul's own fault that he was in jail. Paul could have been more diplomatic. He should have read *How to Win Friends and Influence People.* The young admirers took the case to Paul. Should they try to get that preacher kicked out of the pulpit? What could they do to get revenge?

Paul's answer is a classic: "What does it matter? The important thing is that Christ is preached, whether from false motives or true." To Paul that was the only thing that mattered. What a beautiful lesson in priorities.

What Really Matters?
What Is Really Important?

Two terrific questions to keep our heads in the ballgame: What really matters to you? What's really important? I mean *really* important. Winning the game was more important than arguing a single point. Making a life is more important than making a living.

I've always admired Sheriff Andy Taylor on the Andy Griffith show. Everything Barney Fife, the bumbling deputy, does turns out awful. But what's so beautiful is that Andy always believes in Barney. He always gives him the benefit of the doubt. He lets Barney get the praise for work Andy does. We need more Andy Taylor's in the world. He shows that what matters, what's really important, is friendship, loyalty, and encouragement.

Is it really so important to prove you're right? Do you hang in there until you've won the argument but lost the friend?

Harboring resent-ment is letting a person you despise live in your mind *rent free.*

While we're at it, what about grudges? Well, he did me wrong! And he did it on purpose, the dirty rat. You see lots of this in court battles, divorce cases, and custody fights. In the long run right will win, if you keep your eyes on the right thing. The Bible says, "And we know that all things work together for good to them that love the Lord" (Romans 8:28 KJV).

Harboring resentment is letting a person you despise live in your mind *rent free.* Grudge-bearing is harder on the *grudger* than the *grudgee*, remember? Life is simply too short to be small.

Dave Cone could have used that advice. We've got to look at things over the long run, keeping our eyes on the real objective and the final outcome. To the Christian that objective is Jesus: "Let us fix our eyes on Jesus" (Hebrews 12:2).

Let's keep our heads, our eyes, our hearts, and our passions in the game!

Broccoli Can Kill

George Bush, former president of the United States, and I have at least one thing in common. We both hate broccoli. And I love all that satire and all those jokes about broccoli.

Some guy was doing a piece in a pharmaceutical journal. He noted that nearly all sick people have eaten broccoli and that the effects are cumulative. It's estimated that 99.9 percent of all people who die from cancer have eaten broccoli at least once. About the same amount of those who have been involved in automobile accidents ate broccoli within sixty days before the accident. Suspicious. Mighty suspicious. Some 93.4 percent of juvenile delinquents come from homes where broccoli is served frequently. And get this: among those born between 1820 and 1850 there has been a 100 percent mortality rate among broccoli eaters. Further, all broccoli eaters who were born between 1900 and 1910 today have wrinkled skin, brittle bones, few teeth, and failing eyesight . . . that is, if the perils of broccoli have not already caused their deaths. You can certainly see why George Bush and I do not eat broccoli.

Right Statistics–Wrong Conclusions

There are people who can put two and two together and come up with twenty-two. Sometimes we just don't see the picture clearly.

I'm reminded of the guy who ran a boat rental place. He yelled out, "Boat number ninety-nine, your time's about up. Better bring the boat in."

No answer.

A few minutes later he yelled again. "Boat ninety-nine, your time's up. Get that boat back in here!"

No reply. By this time he was pretty agitated.

At the top of his voice he said, "All right, boat ninety-nine, you're way past time. I'm going to have to charge you double. Get in here now, and I don't mean maybe!"

His hired hand said, "Boss, don't we only have seventy-five boats?"

One more time on the bull horn, "Boat sixty-six, are you having trouble out there?"

A prominent Bishop from England was making his first visit to America, and he wanted to make a good impression. The press asked, "Will you be visiting any of our pubs while you're here?"

The Bishop replied, "*Are* there pubs in America?"

Well the story came out: "Bishop's first question upon arrival in America was 'Are there any pubs in America?'"

Lots of people add up facts but come to wrong conclusions. They read of an airplane crash and announce, "You couldn't pay me to get on an airplane." I read some stats once showing the fatality rates for every million miles traveled via various kinds of transportation. There were thirteen fatalaties per million miles for trains, fourteen for buses, and fifteen for airplanes. Now hold onto your hats. For every million miles traveled by car, *five hundred* were killed!

Exaggeration is a common problem today. We say things like, "I've told you a million times" or, "I'm gonna have to kill that kid!"

A city guy decided to move to the country and commute to work every day. He wanted to live in the great outdoors. So he bought twenty acres with a house and pond, just far enough out of town to escape the noise and hustle and bustle of city life. The first night in the new house he couldn't sleep. The sound of frogs croaking on his pond kept him up all night. But he was an entrepreneur. He knew what frog legs cost, so the next day he approached a restaurant owner in the city. Could he handle about a million pairs of frog legs? Well, *he* couldn't, but he could sure market them to other restaurants in the city and, indeed, across the nation. They made a deal to take all the frog legs he could bring in. The next day the city farmer came in with one scrawny pair of frog legs. "Well," he said, "it *sounded* like a million!"

I was just a young kid, twenty-four years old, when I took my first preaching job in Stockdale, Texas. Its population was 1,100, mostly retired people. We had about a hundred folks in that church. I was long on excitement and short on brains. So their prayer for me was, "Lord, don't let him hurt us, until he learns how to help us." Stockdale had one of those little country stores, with one gas pump, red soda pop, and all that stuff. It was run by an old gentleman by the name of Lee Montgomery. He was a member of the church, so I often went there to talk to Lee and drink red soda pop. Lee was sort of my father confessor.

I preached a sermon one Sunday that didn't go over too well. I began hearing about it, and I was crushed. It was the first time anyone had ever criticized me. I was hurt and mad. I headed for Lee Montgomery's store for some red pop and sympathy.

I told Lee, "I'm quittin'. The whole church is mad at me and I'm leaving!"

Lee looked at me carefully and said, "The whole church is mad at you?"

I said, "That's right. And I'm leaving!"

"Name them."

"What?"

Lee said, "You said the whole church is mad at you. Name them."

I shot back, "Jewel Dacy's mad at me."

"Who else?"

"Leta McGrew's mad at me!"

Lee said, "Yeah, she's really mad at you. Go on."

I tried to add to the list, but I was out of names. And for emphasis Lee said again, "The *whole church* is mad at you." It taught me a valuable lesson about exaggerating.

Never Focus on Negatives!

Many people focus on obstacles or problems and then conclude that the job can't be done. "Hello, is this the Chief of Police? Listen, I need to drive across town today. What time will all the lights be green? I don't want to drive if there are red lights or stop signs. When can I drive across town problem-free?" Can you imagine that? But that's the way some people approach life.

My first book was titled *You Can't Fly to Heaven in a Straight Line*. I pointed out that you can't go anywhere in a straight line. I'm writing this chapter in Alaska. We flew north, south, east, and west to get here. It would have been cheaper and faster if they could just fly here in a straight line. But the runways don't lie that way. And even once you're in the sky, you can't fly to Alaska in a straight line. There's the curvature of the earth and the velocity and direction of the wind. We kept getting blown off course.

But there was a navigator aboard and about a million dollars worth of equipment just to help him navigate. Every time we got blown off course, he just adjusted a knob, pulled a lever, or pressed a button, and the course was corrected.

It's a foregone conclusion that you'll get blown off course. It's not fatal. It's just the way everything works. But this fact of life makes at least three things very important:

1. Decide where you want to go.
2. Make adjustments when blown off course.
3. Just hang in there.

It makes for an exciting and adventurous trip.

Lots of people look at the obstacles. But I'm handicapped. I'm a minority. I'm a woman. I've lost my job. I'm dying. Try laying that reasoning alongside Colin Powell, five-star general in the United States Army. He's the first black person to hold that position. Tell that to Janet Reno, the first woman Attorney General. Shout it back to Franklin Delano Roosevelt, who campaigned successfully for four terms as President of the United States . . . from the wheelchair to which polio had left him bound.

Have you ever said, "This is just not my day"? Well then, *whose day is it?*

> It's a foregone conclusion that you'll get blown off course. It's not fatal. It's just the way everything works.

Reject the Negative— Go with the Positive

Reading negative feedback is especially important. Leaders of the church will sometimes say, "My phone rang off the wall," which means they had maybe six or seven phone calls criticizing something that went on at church.

That's the whole-church-is-mad-at-me syndrome. That's the broccoli-can-kill way of thinking. In a church of a thousand people, it is *good* news when only six or seven people criticize what you're doing. I've heard industry specialists say that "until you have 12 percent of your people upset, it's not a major problem." In a church of a thousand, that's one hundred twenty people. Our elders have *never* had that many people complain about the things we do or the direction we're going. Praise God, we must be on the right track.

Negative people will always be with us. But folks who say it can't be done are constantly being interrupted by the folks who are doing it. So why don't you get on with the positive? Why don't you get in on the being, doing, having, and going? *You* can be the one who gets the breaks, accomplishes the goals, is the success, has a good marriage, builds a great business, raises good kids, grows a great church, benefits mankind, impacts a city, a state, a nation, or a world? Broccoli thinking makes us neurotic. It causes us to miss out on life's great blessings.

Folks who say it can't be done are constantly being interrupted by the folks who are doing it.

Look above the Mess to the Master

Two convicts looked through prison bars.
One saw mud, the other, stars.

It's a question of where you're looking, what you're looking for, and to whom do you look?

The waitress said, "I don't go to church. I've seen all the Christianity I need to see!"

The table full of preachers sat frozen by her reply to an invitation to come to a seminar that night. One preacher put it all in perspective: "Lady, if I had seen what you've seen, I probably wouldn't either."

We've got to look above imperfect people and see Jesus. He loved us when we were unlovable. He saved us when we were unsaveable. He counted us worthy when we were unworthy. If your eyes are on his imperfect followers, you'll never make it. Keep your eyes on Jesus. His is the best way to live, the only way to die.

Now that we've straightened all that out, let's go get something to eat. But if you don't mind, I'll skip the broccoli.

Chapter Fifteen

A Survival Plan for Planet Earth

We hear so much about what we're doing to our environment, our planet, and our universe. It's called the greenhouse effect. We have holes in the ozone layer, air and water pollution, and rivers that catch fire. Our air is even dangerous to breathe.

I asked a friend who lives in California, "What about all that pollution in the air?"

He replied, "I wouldn't trust air I couldn't see!"

We're into recycling paper, glass, and plastic. And we're making biodegradable diapers. Whether at home or abroad, I'm sure we'd like to protect our planet and make our world safer for our children and generations to come. Here are eight suggestions for a better world, starting with me.

1. Recycle Kindness

Surely when a kindness has been done to you, you should pass it on. Get into the habit of returning good for evil too. You know that's what the Lord said. Don't seek revenge. Overcome evil with good. Give plenty of smiles.

Smiling won't solve all your problems, but it will make folks wonder what you've been up to.

I'm a smiler. People often comment that I'm always smiling. I tell them, "It's all the same price. So I choose to smile rather than frown!" Now smiling won't solve all your problems, but it will make folks wonder what you've been up to.

Be thoughtful. Send notes of appreciation. You don't know what to say? Isn't it wonderful we've got Hallmark when you care to send the best? They, and a hundred other companies, always have cards that are just right for special occasions. It's an inexpensive way to recycle kindness and show appreciation and love. Someone said, "The greatest good we can do for others is not just to share our riches with them, but to reveal theirs." It's nice to be important, but it's more important to be nice.

2. Plant a Kiss

Preferably plant it on someone you love or at least on someone you know. Don't be like the poor soul who didn't kiss his wife for twenty years and then shot the man who did.

The Bible talks about kissing. It surprises some people. "Come, my son, and kiss me" (Genesis 27:26). The father ran to the prodigal son. He threw his arms around him and kissed him (Luke 15:20). Five times the Bible says "Greet one another with a kiss of love" (1 Peter 5:14; cf. Romans 16:16; 1 Corinthians 16:20; 2 Corinthians 13:12; 1 Thessalonians 5:26).

A young man courting a young lady is often accused of kissing her too much. "I just can't help myself," he says. Then they marry. Now that he can literally "help himself," kissing diminishes or goes away all together. What a pity!

And of course, make sure your kisses are "holy kisses." Kissing is a language, and we must always be sure we're saying the right thing.

3. Stop Air Pollution

I can't do much about the giant problem of polluting the air. Oh, I don't fill my car with gas on ozone alert days, and I keep my cars tuned up so few exhaust fumes contaminate the air. But I can do something about the pollution of gossip, cursing, pessimism, and put downs. I'm talking about unnecessary criticism, tearing up another's ribbon, or raining on someone else's parade. I like those signs on cigarette packages: "Smoking is injurious to your health." Somewhere we ought to post signs that read, "Negative talk is injurious to your health."

It takes approximately eleven positive statements to overcome the effect of one negative. And some people look for faults in others as if there were a reward for finding them. Remember the old, simple slogan, "If you can't say something nice, don't say anything at all." The Bible says, "Do everything without complaining or arguing" (Philippians 2:14).

We ought to get tough on polluters. I don't think we'll ever put pornographers out of business. But we can do a good job of *self*-censorship. They can't sell it if we don't buy it. Paul Harvey once said, "Movies that are harmful to children for moral reasons are harmful to adults for the same reason."

4. Conserve Water

Don't cause tears by your thoughtless words and actions. We have no right to hurt others. I used to tell bald jokes and fat jokes. There's a lot of "good" material about bald and fat people. When I told those jokes, people would laugh, and that encouraged me to tell them again another time. Then someone gave me a definition of *funny* that changed a lot of my material: "Unless *everyone* is laughing, it's not funny." You see, if someone in your audience is offended by humor at their expense, it's not funny!

Don't pat someone's stomach and remark, "You're putting on a little weight I see." Don't comment that someone is becoming a little bald. Dry others' tears with your understanding and compassion. Ask yourself, "Can I make it better? Can I do something to make them feel okay?" Those who can, have a great gift from God. You see, love seeks the best interest of the person loved.

5. Consume Less

I'm talking here of things that hurt you. Americans are digging their graves with their own teeth and their lifestyles. I preach too many unnecessary funerals because of the big four: obesity, eating wrong, stress, and a sedentary lifestyle. Add smoking, alcohol, and other unnecessary drugs to those, and you have a lethal combination. The Surgeon General's warning on the back of that cigarette package is not on there to ruin your fun. It's to promote health, happiness, and long life. Pay attention here. You'll be the winner—you and those who love you.

6. Control Your Use of Plastic

I'm talking about the great American curse—*credit cards.* You can buy anything for nothing down and only four hundred painless payments. Americans are finding out those payments aren't as painless as they're cracked up to be.

Larry Burkett is a foremost money management consultant. He says the best thing that could happen to our credit cards is to heat the oven to 500 degrees and insert the cards. He's not really against credit cards, but he teaches that you must control them or they will control you. He gives three rules for safe use of credit cards:

1. Don't charge what you have not budgeted for.
2. Pay the card off in full each month.
3. The day you get a bill that you can't pay off in full, tear up your card. You've just proven you can't handle it correctly.

Never give anyone the power to affect the peace and harmony of your life.

I am persuaded that following these rules would keep a lot of people out of a lot of trouble. And don't co-sign loans. Doing so guarantees that you will make payments if the party you signed for doesn't. Be generous in sharing what you *do* have. Be stingy in sharing what you *do not* have.

The Bible tells you plainly *not* to co-sign loans. (Read Proverbs 6:1–5.)

7. Enhance Global Warming

Our world is a cold place. There's a shortage of love, warm caring, and affection. Sometimes a person will say to me, "I'm just not an affectionate person." Get over it! Show a little love. Give affectionate hugs. Share warm fuzzies. Tolerate each other's differences. It's okay to garden organically, but leave the fertilizer in the yard. It has no place in relationships. Don't dump garbage or bring refuse into your marriage. Don't be touchy and testy in your dealings with others. Give large doses of love, acceptance, and forgiveness. Praise much; criticize little. Offer forgiveness liberally and continually. If you are strong on your "rights," be equally strong on other people's rights.

8. Give the Planet Owner a Chance

Acknowledge that creation proves there's a creator. Design demands a designer. The most logical, provable statement in the Bible is the first one, "In the beginning God created the heavens and the earth" (Genesis 1:1). Acclaim his ownership of what he has made. "The earth is the Lord's, and everything in it" (Psalm 24:1). Assume he knows best. Applaud his sovereignty, and accept his blessings.

These steps will keep our planet warm, at least where you live. It will give you the best of *now* and the best of *eternity.*

Chapter Sixteen

Are You a Hot Dog or Just a Weenie?

Harry had a thriving hot dog stand. It was in a good location, and he served good products. There were lots of hungry people, and he did very well.

Harry was hard of hearing, so he had no radio. His eyesight wasn't any good either, so he didn't read the newspapers or watch TV. But he sold good hot dogs. He had signs out on the highway telling travelers how good they were. He stood there at his little stand by the side of the road yelling, "Anybody want to buy a *good* hot dog?" They *were* good, and the people bought them. So, he bought more meat and buns. Then he bought a better stove to handle more sales. Things were going great!

Harry had a son with a college degree paid for by the profits of his thriving hot dog business. His son majored in economics. The son said, "Dad, haven't you been listening to the radio? Haven't you been reading the papers? Our country is facing one of the biggest recessions in its history. There's trouble in the Middle East, and we've got a three trillion dollar deficit in our national debt. On the home front we have riots, inflation, pollution, strikes, minorities, the poor, drugs, fascists, and communists. Dad, you've got to get ready for this recession. Stop spending so much money on advertising and equipment. Cut down on the size of your hot dog buns and weenies. This way you'll be ahead when the recession hits."

Harry's son had a college degree in economics. He kept up with all the latest statistics and trends. He ought to know what he was talking about. Harry was so glad he had a son to help him get ready for this recession. He did everything his son advised him to do. And sure enough, when the recession came, Harry was ready. But he couldn't understand why the hot dog stand around the corner was doing better than he was. They were spending lots of money on advertising and were putting out good-sized hot dogs with everything on them. They were buying better equipment and taking home larger profits.

Most depressions are man made, friends.

Your Life Becomes What Your Mind Is Fed

I attended the first Positive Mental Attitude rally in Kansas City in 1978. Speakers included Dr. Norman Vincent Peale, Zig Ziglar, Cavett Robert, and Paul Harvey. It was fantastic. They said things like, "What your mind can conceive and believe, your life can achieve."

I was turned on. It wasn't a religious rally, but I realized I could put book, chapter, and verse to everything they were saying. The apostle Paul said, "I can do everything through him who gives me strength" (Philippians 4:13).

Zig Ziglar would have called Harry a "SNIOP" (Susceptible to the Negative Influence of Other People).

The Negative, Garbage-Dumping Game

We live in a negative, garbage-dumping world. Everyday in a myriad of ways negatives are poured into your life. Through movies and TV, books and magazines, you are constantly bombarded with a barrage of negative thinking, scandal, crime, greed, and lust. The heroes are either in trouble, headed for trouble, or have just gotten out of trouble. The world is shown to be a corrupt place, where you've got to fight fire with fire or wrong with wrong. And too often, you can't tell the good guys from the bad guys.

A coworker says, "Shirley, you look awful." Bolster that with a couple of other people telling her the same thing, and she goes home sick by noon. Parents say to their kids, "You'll never amount to anything," or "You'll be the death of me yet." Physical and sexual abuse are terrible, but so are emotional and verbal abuse. They have the same effect—the result is poor self-esteem. The victim is programmed for failure and fear, which show up in broken marriages, loss of jobs, and the inability to have healthy relationships.

It Can also Work Positively

How about "banquet dumping" instead of "garbage dumping"? It's GIGO— garbage in, garbage out. Pour in praise, compliments, and encouragement instead of negativism. The outcome will be as dramatic as garbage dumping, except with the opposite result.

The apostle Paul is a classic example of a positive attitude that came from positive feedback. Listen to these glorious words:

> Rejoice in the Lord always. I will say it again: Rejoice! Let your gentleness be evident to all. The Lord is near. Do not be anxious about anything, but in everything, by prayer and petition, with thanksgiving, present your requests to God. And the peace of God, which transcends all understanding, will guard your hearts and your minds in Christ Jesus. (Philippians 4:4–7)

Can you believe Paul was in prison at the time he wrote those exhilarating words? The food was bad, and the treatment was worse. Prospects for the future were dim. Yet he was rejoicing. What could make Paul feel positive and radiant in the midst of such circumstances?

Paul was practicing his banquet thinking. Sure he was in jail, but he was also a child of God. He remembered that personal encounter on the road to Damascus with Jesus Christ. He was saved from his past sins and added to the family of God. Paul now had a Father, a family (the church), a fellowship, and a future. And he enjoyed the indwelling of the Holy Spirit. Prison could not take that away from him, and he wasn't going to let it spoil his attitude. Even if they killed him, it would only launch him right into the presence of God to live in eternity with Jesus Christ and the saved of the ages. Banquet thinking made him a positive thinker. It affected his current performance and gave substance to his hope for the future.

Be Careful of Loser's Limp

Jerry Rice, great receiver for the San Francisco Forty Niners, maneuvers in behind the defensive back. Steve Young's pass is on the money, and the defensive back knows he's beaten, but he chases Rice to no avail. It's a touchdown for sure. So what does the back do? He pulls up limping, which gains the sympathy of the crowd. Shucks, no wonder he didn't catch Rice. The poor fellow is crippled. It covered his mistake and gave him an excuse not to look bad.

There are lots of loser's limps in life, such as blaming other people or blaming the country or the times. I would have made it, *but.* . . . The fault is not with America. Our country has a lot of problems, prejudices, and inequality. But it's way ahead of whatever is in second place. Plenty of Americans make it in spite of the obstacles. If you can't make it in America, it's unlikely you could make it anywhere else. Ask any immigrant. They're the ones who really know the opportunity our country provides.

The fault is not with the times. We've had depression, recession, inflation, bad markets, job shortages, and corruption in high places. While some people are blaming circumstances for their failure, others are making it to the top *in the same circumstances.*

The fault is not with your heritage. You say, "I had the wrong parents, I'm the wrong sex, wrong age, wrong color, and I have room-temperature IQ." Study successes. There is no pattern. No set of circumstances has to be in place for success to occur.

Some people make it while others don't. It has a lot more to do with attitude than heritage. A little boy watched a balloon man at the fair. Every now and then he'd release a balloon. As it soared up into the sky, people would notice, gather around and buy balloons. He released a yellow one. Then a white one. Then a red one. The little boy approached the man.

"Mister," he said, "if you released a black balloon, would it go as high as the others?"

> Our country has a lot of problems. But it's way ahead of whatever is in second place.

123

"Son," the balloon man answered, "it isn't the color of the balloon that makes it go so high. It's the stuff on the inside!"

Four Steps to Becoming a "Hot Dog"

I'm assuming that you don't want to be a weenie. You want to be a "hot dog." *Step one* is to develop a positive self-image. Accept the fact that you've been made in the image of God. Feed your mind with the good, the clean, the pure, and the powerful. Read good books. Listen to good tapes. Only watch good movies. Associate with positive people. Read your Bible—it's the handbook for all positive literature. It says, "Everything is possible for him who believes" (Mark 9:23).

Step two is to learn to receive through giving. The Bible says, "Give and it will be given to you. A good measure, pressed down, shaken together and running over, will be poured into your lap. For with the measure you use, it will be measured to you" (Luke 6:38).

This is a promise of God, and it applies to anything. You want trouble? Just give it, and you'll get plenty back. But suppose you want love, happiness, a good relationship, better friends, more money, and better health? Give those things to others, and watch them come home a hundred fold to you. You can get anything in life you want if you just help enough other people get what they want.

Persist! That's *step three*. I love the poster with the cat hanging from a stick. Both paws are gripping the stick. His eyes are wide with apprehension. And the caption says, "Hang in there, baby!" Remember, a big shot is just a little shot that kept shooting.

Brett Hart tells the story of a miner who had suffered years of failure. He finally drove his pick in the ground, sold his claim for a song, and gave up. The new owner, in the process of pulling the pick out of the ground, discovered traces of gold. The old miner had just given up too soon. There are all kinds of successes just around the corner for the one who will not give up. Again, listen to the Word of God: "Let us not become weary in doing good, for at the proper time we will reap a harvest if we do not give up" (Galatians 6:9).

And finally, *step four,* commit your plans (life) to the Lord. "Commit to the Lord whatever you do, and your plans will succeed" (Proverbs 16:3). David made this discovery in the Psalms: "I was young and now I am old, yet I have never seen the righteous forsaken or their children begging bread" (Psalm 37:25).

Harry should have known these steps. He could have been a hot dog. Instead he wound up being a weenie. Now it's your turn to choose!

Chapter
Seventeen

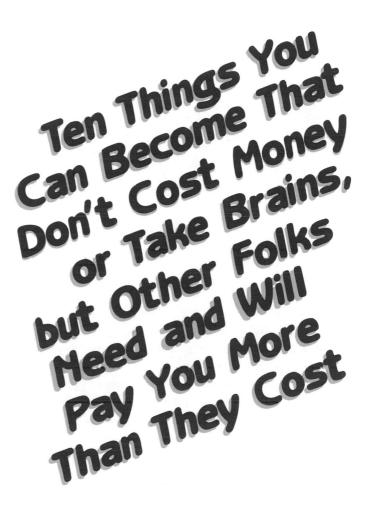

Ten Things You Can Become That Don't Cost Money or Take Brains, but Other Folks Need and Will Pay You More Than They Cost

This chapter is a case where the title is longer than the text. But I think we'll have a lot of fun with it. If you can have fun while learning valuable lessons about life, you're way ahead in my opinion.

Let's start by dissecting that marathon title:

"Things you can become": These are things you want to become.

"Don't cost money": Everyone can afford these things.

"Don't take brains": Everyone is smart enough to do them.

"Other folks need": There's a good market for what you become.

"Pays you more than they cost": Bottom line profit.

Ready? Here's how to do it.

1. Become a Healer

We can all probably be classified as healers or hurters. And there are far too many hurters in the world today. Some people hurt others with guns and knives. Some hurt with words and put downs. Some make things better; some make matters worse. Lecturing about morality to a pregnant teenager is too late, but healing a lost, hurting girl can still be done.

The good Samaritan story in Luke 10:25–37 is a case in point. I'm not sure we should call him the *good* Samaritan. His behavior ought to reflect the *normal* Samaritan. We should all play his role. Jesus was trying to explain how we should treat our neighbors. So he told about a mugging. A man was beaten, robbed, and left for dead beside the road. Three people happened along in succession. The first was a priest. That was fortunate . . . wasn't it? Now you *know* a priest would help. But no! He didn't want to get involved. It would probably make him late for an appointment. He might mess up his suit. He crossed the street and passed the man by.

A Levite was next. Perhaps he looked at his watch and just didn't have time for this. It wasn't his fault the man was in trouble. Besides, no one would know. He, too, passed by.

And then a Samaritan came by. Remember, the Samaritans were on the bottom end of the social totem pole. No one would help *him* if he were the one lying there. But he had pity on the man. He bandaged his wounds, put the injured man on his own donkey, and took him into town. He took him to a Holiday Inn, registered him there for recovery, and put it all on his own credit card, saying, "If he needs to stay longer, just add it to my bill." And Jesus said, "Go and do likewise."

"Brothers, if someone is caught in a sin, you who are spiritual should restore him gently. But watch yourself, or you also may be tempted. Carry each other's burdens, and in this way you will fulfill the law of Christ" (Galatians 6:1–2).

2. Be an Encourager

Romans 12:5–8 lists seven gifts God has distributed to his people. Among them is the gift of encouragement. It surely belongs at the top of the list. It is so needed today. Barnabas was called "Son of Encouragement" (Acts 4:36). He played his part well. He and Paul were selected by the Holy Spirit to travel to Asia to preach the Good News about Jesus.

Barnabas had a nephew named John Mark. Barnabas encouraged John to go with them on the trip. But difficulty arose. We're not told what it was. Perhaps the going was just too tough or maybe Mark just got homesick. He finally quit and returned home.

When Paul and Barnabas got ready to go on the next trip, Barnabas wanted to take Mark again, but Paul refused. He wouldn't take a quitter. So they split. Barnabas took Mark, and Paul chose a new partner, Silas. We don't hear from John Mark again until years later. Paul was in prison, writing to Timothy with instructions about coming to visit him. He said, "Get Mark and bring him with you, because he is helpful to me in my ministry" (2 Timothy 4:11).

Some people seem to have the knack of showing you where you went wrong. Others have the gift of encouraging you to do better, to try again.

We thank God for the Barnabases in this world—those who keep believing in us. They tell us we can do it. They are heavy on compassion and are ready with a helping hand when we fall.

Many of the greatest successes of our day would not be where they are if not for an encourager in their lives. It doesn't cost money to be an encourager. It's so needed. And it pays great dividends.

3. Be a Listener

A business representative was on an out-of-town trip. Late that night from his hotel room, he put in a call to his wife. To his surprise his four-year-old son answered the phone.

"Bobby, what are you doing up this hour? Tell your mom I want to talk to her."

"She's asleep."

"Go wake her up, Son. Daddy needs to talk to her."

"I can't wake her up, Dad. She's been asleep all day. Her eyes are open, and they look funny."

The frantic father shouted, "Bobby, hang up the phone so Daddy can get someone there to help."

And Bobby screamed back at his dad, "Daddy, don't hang up on me!"

Lots of people in our world feel hung up on. They think no one cares. One guy advertised in the paper, "I'll listen to your troubles—thirty dollars per call." And he got lots of takers.

Communication, or the lack of it, is behind most of the hurts in the world. Do you ever feel as if you're not getting through or that you're not really being heard? It's estimated that husbands and wives spend about thirty-seven minutes per week talking to each other. And how much time is spent talking to your kids? I don't mean small talk, but really talking, asking how they're doing, listening for an answer, really trying to understand what they are saying and where they are coming from. If you really want to do something that doesn't cost money or take brains, that other folks need and will pay for . . . become a listener.

4. Be a Hugger

A hugger has been defined as an encourager with arms. We can encourage from a distance, but it takes a warm, close body to hug and give warm fuzzies. There's such value in touch. We now know that if a child is not held, touched, and caressed in the first year of its life, it will die. I have a "Hugger/Huggee" line in my Peak of the Week class on Wednesday nights. I ask for volunteer huggers to come stand beside me. Then I give the audience two minutes to come through the hugging line. It's a wonderful time.

All kinds of people get in line. People who get plenty of affection from their families and friends get in line. Our widow ladies get in line. Our singles are especially good about getting in line. Even little children get in line. There's a song that says, "I need someone to hold me when I cry." The truth is we need warm hugs for lots of reasons. Hugs reassure us that we're lovable. Hugs congratulate us. Hugs say, "I care." Hugs encourage us when we've had a rough day.

Hugs are inexpensive, they don't take long to give, they take no training to learn, and they don't take much effort or expend much energy.

> A hugger has been defined as an encourager with arms.

Yet they pay such great dividends. Scripture says, "Be kindly affectioned one to another" (Romans 12:10 KJV).

On one occasion a man with leprosy said to Jesus, "Lord, if you are willing, you can make me clean." Jesus reached out and touched him. Immediately he was cleansed from his terrible disease.

That takes a bit of looking at. Leprosy is a horrible skin disease. It's nasty, and there are secretions. Jesus didn't have to touch him. He could have healed him from across the room. But Jesus touched him because he knew the value of touch.

Another time people brought little children to Jesus to have him touch them. The disciples misunderstood. The master was busy teaching. These kids were in the way. And they rebuked the people for the distraction. But Jesus said, "Let the little children come to me, and do not hinder them, for the kingdom of God belongs to such as these." And he took the children in his arms. He put his hands on them and blessed them.

And then there's that wonderful story we call the prodigal son. A boy ran away from home. He played the fool and ended up in the pig pen. The saloon became his salvation. But he finally woke up and decided to go home to his father. He was dirty, hungry, and miserable. But while he was still a long way from home, his father saw him coming. The father was filled with compassion. He *ran* to his boy and threw his arms around him and kissed him. It was a marvelous reunion. Thank God for a loving, hugging Jesus!

Give plenty of hugs. They don't cost money. They don't take brains. Anyone can do it. Other people need them. And they will pay more than they cost.

> Give plenty of hugs. They don't cost money or take brains. Anyone can do it, and other people need them.

5. Be a Lover

The people wanted to know about the *Readers' Digest Bible*. They said, "Lord, this is a big, thick book. We don't think we can absorb it all or get it all done. Isn't there a simpler way to put all this?" And to their surprise Jesus gave them a short cut.

> "Love the Lord your God with all your heart and with all your soul and with all your mind." This is the first and greatest commandment. And the second is like it: "Love your neighbor as yourself." All the Law and the Prophets hang on these two commandments. (Matthew 22:37–40)

Church members seem to always be preoccupied with the identity of the church. It must wear the right name, be organized in the right way, be known for its teachings on such topics as the Holy Spirit, marriage and divorce, and a million other things. Again Jesus provides a short cut: "A new command I give you: Love one another. As I have loved you, so you must love one another. By this all men will know that you are my disciples, if you love one another" (John 13:34–35).

Our God is a lover. "For God so loved" is the golden text of the Bible. Romans, chapter eight, begins with "no condemnation," ends with "no separation," and in the middle shouts "glory!" Nothing can separate us from the love of God:

> For I am convinced that neither death nor life, neither angels nor demons, neither the present nor the future, nor any powers, neither height nor depth, nor anything else in all creation, will be able to separate us from the love of God that is in Christ Jesus our Lord. (Romans 8:38–39)

Be a lover. Love seeks the best interest of its object. Love is a choice. Are you a person of love? Tell it. Show it. Live it. You can become a lover. It doesn't cost money. It doesn't take brains. Other people need your love. And it will pay you dividends.

6. Be a Forgiver

Grudge bearing is harder on the "grudger" than the "grudgee." Forgive people because they need it. Forgive because *you* need it. Forgive when they did it to you on purpose. Forgive your ex-husband or ex-wife. Forgive your children for failing you. Forgive your parents; they failed you too.

Jesus taught forgiveness. He said, "For if you forgive men when they sin against you, your heavenly Father will also forgive you. But if you do not forgive men their sins, your Father will not forgive your sins" (Matthew 6:14–15).

Peter thought he had it on straight. He said, "Lord, how many times shall I forgive my brother when he sins against me? Up to seven times?" And Jesus' classic answer was, "Not seven times, but seventy-seven times" (Matthew 18:21–22). In other words, be a perpetual forgiver.

The crowning example of forgiveness is in Jesus' words on the cross: "Father, forgive them; for they know not what they do" (Luke 23:34). I want to scream out, "Oh yes they did know what they were doing!" But forgiving is what Jesus was doing on Calvary. Be a forgiver. What dividends it pays! People need it so badly, and it doesn't cost; it pays.

7. Be a Helper

God's conversation with Moses in Exodus chapter four is a classic. The time was ripe to remove the Jewish people from Egyptian slavery. God picked Moses to lead them out. But Moses was full of excuses: "They won't listen to me." "I'm not a good speaker." "Please send someone else."

God reassured Moses of his divine help. He also gave him Aaron as his personal helper with the task. The result was the rescue of the Israelite nation and the subsequent coming of Jesus Christ into the world. God isn't going to leave any of us without help.

The Book of Nehemiah tells of the rebuilding of the wall of Jerusalem. There were opposing armies who didn't want the job done. The walls were built in spite of enormous obstacles. One of the keys to their success is seen in the expression, "next to him" (mentioned eleven times in Nehemiah 3). They helped each other. One took over where the other one left off. Many hands make light work. And in this case, this "helping" provided fellowship, encouragement, security, and faith.

Be a helper. Volunteer to do works of service. Don't you just love to see elderly people volunteering at hospitals? And I love the candy stripers, young teenage boys and girls, giving freely of their time to help others. It's also great to see the same spirit in our churches—people giving freely and generously of their time, talents, and treasures in the work of God. This is the way to happiness and success.

8. Be a Believer

I love Kenny Rogers' song, "She believes in me." It's the story of a night club singer who works long hours for not much pay. Did he get it right tonight? Will they ask him back? He comes home late from work. His wife wakes up and reassures him that she believes in him, and that's all he needs to get out there and give it one more try.

We all need people to believe in us. I preach for one of the finest churches in the nation. The road to this place was rocky. There were so many times I wanted to quit. I've made all the mistakes in the book—and a lot that are not in the book. Certain editors have assailed me with accusations that I am inadequate and off track. My reply has always been that if they knew the really tough things I struggle with, they wouldn't fool around with those little things they shoot at me about.

So what keeps us going? How do we hang in there and keep trying when the circumstances all around us scream at us to quit? It's the folks who believe in us and write little notes to that affect that keep us going. I've learned that God arranges for you to get these notes at just the time you need them most.

The "love chapter," 1 Corinthians 13, says that love "believeth all things" (v. 7 KJV). Love gives the benefit of doubt. Love chooses to believe that its loved ones are all right, that they can make it, that they are somehow worth something. Without that belief, none of us will make it. The achievers of this world are so in debt to the believers. Thanks for believing in us.

9. Be a Supporter

Professional basketball teams are pretty much alike. They hire the best players. The players sign million-dollar contracts. On any given day one team can beat another. But there is one factor that wins more games than any other. It is called "home-court advantage." Teams win most of the games that are played "at home," in front of their own fans. Now the court is the same size. The ball is the same size and weight. The basket is the same height. There is absolutely no difference in playing in one gymnasium or another. But teams win consistently in front of their own fans—their supporters, their boosters.

A supporter is one who stands by your side, who cheers you on to victory. And they *do* cheer. Sometimes it's deafening! There is power in the home-court advantage. Teams are brought to peak performance. They just win more in front of their own supporters.

It would be wonderful if we realized the power in this. People need to root for their home teams. But they also ought to support their communities. Communities taught to support one another can stamp out drug traffic in their neighborhoods. They can reduce crime and provide a safer environment for one another.

It works that way for families too. Husbands and wives should be one another's greatest cheerleaders. Parents should boost their kids.

You can't *drive* your kids anywhere. But you can *praise* them into greatness. Kids should know that their greatest fans are their parents. And kids should boost their parents too. What a difference it would make if everyone in the family really supported one another.

Be a supporter for your local church too. I'll never understand why people keep going to a particular church year after year but are always critical of every thing going on in the church. They bad-mouth the preacher and disagree with every decision the leaders make. They are generally unhappy. I'll never know why they don't find somewhere else to go where they can really get in and be happy. Perhaps it's because they never really learned how to be a supporter. Changing churches wouldn't help. They just don't know how to boost, support, and encourage their local churches. Maybe it's like one member said, "Pardon me for criticizing, but I have to do what I do best." Ouch!

Be a supporter. It doesn't cost money. It doesn't take brains. Other folks need our support. And it will pay you far more than you'll ever spend.

> You can't *drive* your kids anywhere. But you can *praise* them into greatness.

10. Be a Saver

You can save a lot of things. But I'm refering especially to bringing lost people to Jesus. Do you remember

Andrew's first action after finding Jesus? The Bible says, "The first thing Andrew did was to find his brother Simon and tell him, 'We have found the Messiah' (that is, the Christ). And he brought him to Jesus" (John 1:41–42).

Bringing another person to Jesus is the greatest work in the world. Jesus left heaven and came to earth to reconcile people to God. "The Son of man came to seek and to save the lost" (Luke 19:10 RSV). Jesus instructs us to bring people to him in the command we call the Great Commission.

> Therefore go and make disciples of all nations, baptizing them in the name of the Father and of the Son and of the Holy Spirit, and teaching them to obey everything I have commanded you. And surely I am with you always, to the very end of the age. (Matthew 28:19–20)

When a teenage Christian boy leads a teenage girl to Christ, it's a greater work than anything the United Nations can do, and it's the only thing that finally matters. Be a saver! Think of precious friends who do not know Jesus as Lord and friend. Get into the business of saving others. The Bible says, "He who wins souls is wise" (Proverbs 11:30).

Isn't it nice to know that you can become all these things? They are worthwhile things too. And they don't cost money or take brains. Yet they are the most needed items on the human agenda.

Real personal success and happiness will pour into the lives of anyone who really applies himself to these things.

Well, don't just stand there. Get busy.

Chapter Eighteen

It Was Spring, but I Wanted Summer

Jason Lehman wrote the following free verse, and it is reprinted by permission. It was sent to Dear Abby by his grandmother. He was fourteen at the time he wrote it.

Present Tense

> It was spring.
> But it was summer I wanted.
> The warm days,
> And the great outdoors.
> It was summer.
> But it was fall I wanted.
> The colorful leaves,
> And the cool, dry air.
> It was fall.

But it was winter I wanted.
The beautiful snow,
And the joy of the holiday season.
It was winter.
But it was spring I wanted.
The warmth,
And the blossoming of nature.
I was a child,
But it was adulthood I wanted.
The freedom,
And the respect.
I was 20,
But it was 30 I wanted.
To be mature,
And sophisticated.
I was middle-aged,
But it was 20 I wanted.
The youth,
And the free spirit.
I was retired,
But it was middle-aged I wanted.
The presence of mind,
Without limitations.
My life was over,
But I never got what I wanted.

Discontentment Is a
Very Real Problem Today

People seem to always want something they don't have. They want to be something they're not. They never seem content with what they have or what they are. They see another person whose life seems ideal, and they wish they could trade places. But that ideal person wishes he could trade places with someone else.

It Was Spring, but I Wanted Summer

There are women who wish they were men and men who wish they were women. Older people wish they could turn back the clock: "If I had known then what I know now . . . If I had it to do all over again . . . If I could live my life over . . ." Young people wish they were older. They say, "No one listens to me. Everyone thinks I'm a kid."

There are poor people who wish they were rich. "Oh, what I'd do if I just had the money to do it." It reminds me of the fellow who approached the late Joe Louis, heavy weight boxing champion. "Mr. Louis," he said, "if I were you, I'd go out in the woods and find me the biggest bear I could find and beat him to a pulp!"

Louis replied, "There are bears out there *your* size."

While it may be hard for us to imagine, there are rich people who wish they were poor. "I had a lot less problems then. I knew who my friends were before I had money. Now, everyone is after my money." They find that money cannot buy happiness or true success. Riches bring problems and stress. Prosperity brings enemies who are out to destroy them. The distance between them and their wives is obvious; they are alienated from their kids. And they believe they might have been happy if only they had been poor.

What *is* the best time of life? What *is* the best age? What's the best place to live or the best job to have? Remember that old line "Take this job and shove it"? I saw a baseball cap that read "I wish I had a job to shove."

What Discontentment Brings

Discontentment brings complaining. We're treated like dirt. We feel like an appendage to the body of life. No one really cares about us. So we complain about the system, the government, politicians, the church. Name it and we complain about it. We gripe about the school, the police, and other people. And we even complain about ourselves.

Just because you had a lousy childhood is no excuse for becoming a lousy adult.

Wallace Kelly was our oldest church elder. He's with the Lord now, but he was a positive thinker. He used to say, "Some people would complain if they had a piece of pie in each hand." I think I've met a few of these. It's like these two lines:

When it's cold, we want it hot,
We're always wanting what it's not!

And complaining gets you nowhere. It's like racing your engine with your back wheels jacked up. You hear a lot of noise, but you don't go anywhere.

Discontentment causes blaming. If you're unhappy about something, the next thing is to find someone you can blame. So you blame your mate, your kids, your parents, the church, the school, your friends, or the weather. I've seen people continue to blame their parents for their own failures twenty years after their parents' death. Just because you had a lousy childhood is no excuse for becoming a lousy adult.

Discontentment Is a Killer

Discontented people live with anxiety. They are not happy and cannot look on the bright side, so they constantly feel stressed out, and stress is the number one killer in America. It's connected to strokes, heart attacks, high blood pressure, and hypertension. It contributes to migraines, colitis, and other major and minor irritations. Sooner or later it's going to get you if you don't do something about it.

Discontented people completely ignore the possibilities. With folded arms they *wish* things were different. Their whole future is built on the way they wish things were. They refuse to face reality, missing the beautiful potential that exists for every person in every circumstance of life.

The Keys to Contentment

Play the cards you are dealt. This is another way of saying, "Bloom where you're planted." What you are is God's gift to you. What you become is your gift to God!

Accept yourself. The apostle Paul says, "But in fact God has arranged the parts in the body, every one of them, just as he wanted them to be" (1 Corinthians 12:18).

Act yourself into the feeling. Dale Carnegie used to say, "To get the feeling, you've got to grab the feeling." Psychologist Jerome Bruner put it this way: "You are more likely to act yourself into the feeling, than feel yourself into the acting." We are all manufacturers. Some make good; some make trouble; others only make excuses. If you have tried and failed, it's vastly better than if you do not try, and succeed.

The golden rule says, "Do to others as you would have them do to you" (Luke 6:31). It has been committed to memory, and it needs to be committed to life.

You'll find when you go ahead and play the role you should play, the feeling will come. Feeling good always comes from doing right.

Know your needs and keep them simple. Some people's needs are always changing.

> From eighteen to thirty-five
> a girl needs good looks.
> From thirty-five to fifty-five
> She needs a good personality.
> From fifty-five on she needs cash.

Some people don't know their needs. I had to laugh at one guy's definition of an NFL football game. He said it was "Fifty thousand people who need exercise, watching twenty-two men who need rest."

Author Leo Buscaglia claims our basic needs are food, water, shelter, and clothes. Beyond that we need to love someone worth loving and to hold on to something big enough to hold us. We need to live within our income. We need to become a part of something bigger than ourselves.

Build your hopes on things eternal. A grand old gospel song says,

Time is filled with swift transition—
Naught of earth unmoved can stand—
Build your hopes on things eternal,
Hold to God's unchanging hand.

Many people find that the more they get what they want, the less they want what they get.

In Luke 12, Jesus was speaking to a large crowd. Some agitated person in his audience interrupted him and said, "Tell my brother to divide the inheritance with me." Jesus' response was to caution him against greed. He said a man's life is more than *things*. There are more important issues than "getting what's coming to you." Many people find that the more they get what they want, the less they want what they get.

Then Jesus told a parable—an earthly story with a heavenly meaning. A certain farmer was really prosperous. He harvested a bumper crop every year. Barns bulging with grain, his biggest problem was where to put all his goods. He finally hit on a solution: build bigger barns to make more storage space. Then he felt secure to face the coming years. But Jesus said, "You fool. This very night your life will be demanded from you. Then who will get what you have prepared for yourself?" And his conclusion? "This is how it will be with anyone who stores up things for himself but is not rich toward God" (Luke 12:20–21).

Paul wrote,

It Was Spring, but I Wanted Summer

I have learned to be content whatever the circumstances. I know what it is to be in need, and I know what it is to have plenty. I have learned the secret of being content in any and every situation, whether well fed or hungry, whether living in plenty or in want. I can do everything through him who gives me strength. (Philippians 4:11–13)

And again, "But godliness with contentment is great gain. For we brought nothing into the world, and we can take nothing out of it" (1 Timothy 6:6–7).

Godliness is the key. It brings contentment. Jesus satisfies. The two add up to "great gain."

Jesus wants you to enjoy the spring. But the summer that follows is magnificent. And the fall with its crispness and harvest is delightful; it's pure enjoyment. And even winter is beautiful in its own right. Enjoy every season, every stage of life. Every change is a step up the trail to the top of the mountain. And then we'll take that final leap and reach out and touch the face of God.

Chapter Nineteen

The Fresh Breeze of Integrity

It was a lovely autumn day in Columbus, Ohio. The Metropolitan Armored truck was tooling along Interstate-71. The interstate was bustling with traffic. Unknown to the driver and guard in the truck, the rear door suddenly swung open. Money began pouring out like the first snow of the season. Bills of all denominations filled the air and floated onto the highway and adjacent area—hundreds of thousands of dollars. The money continued to pour out for more than a mile before the guard figured out what had happened.

As the armored car drove out of sight, an estimated two hundred cars converged on the scene. People began scooping it up like kids gathering snow to build a snowman. More than a million dollars was lost.

Melvin Kiser, Ohio Bell Telephone technician, scooped up a sack containing $57,000 in small bills. He later gave it back and was rewarded with a citation and 10 percent of his find. Larry Bromagen, a high school social studies teacher, said a debate broke out in the teachers' lounge about what they would have done with the money. Radio station WXGT asked listeners to call in and say whether they would have kept the money or given it back. Over 61 percent said they would have kept the money. Another station took a similar survey, and 90 percent said they would have kept the cash.

What would you do? Who would know the difference? It wasn't your fault the money flew out of the truck. They're probably covered by insurance anyway. No one would be hurt. What's the *right* thing to do? Would a fresh breeze of integrity make a difference?

Our World Has an Integrity Shortage

We have an epidemic of business executives who skim company funds for personal use to support opulent, immoral lifestyles. Television evangelists won't reveal their financial records. Highly visible religious and secular leaders raise money for one purpose and use it for another. Politicians accept bribes. Athletes shave points, take steroids, throw fights, and shoot cocaine. Mates cheat on one another in illicit affairs. Students cheat on tests. Church leaders steal, lie, defraud, and misuse. Our world could certainly use a fresh breeze of integrity.

What Does the Bible Say?

Let's let our fingers walk through the pages of the Bible:

> Use honest scales and honest weights. (Leviticus 19:36)

The Fresh Breeze of Integrity

A truthful witness gives honest testimony, but a false witness tells lies. (Proverbs 12:17)

Kings take pleasure in honest lips; they value a man who speaks the truth. (Proverbs 16:13)

An honest answer is like a kiss on the lips. (Proverbs 24:26)

Again, you have heard that it was said to the people long ago, "Do not break your oath, but keep the oaths you have made to the Lord." But I tell you, Do not swear at all: either by heaven, for it is God's throne; or by the earth, for it is his footstool; or by Jerusalem, for it is the city of the Great King. And do not swear by your head, for you cannot make even one hair white or black. Simply let your "Yes" be "Yes," and your "No," "No"; anything beyond this comes from the evil one. (Matthew 5:33–37)

Do not repay anyone evil for evil. Be careful to do what is right in the eyes of everybody. (Romans 12:17)

For we are taking pains to do what is right, not only in the eyes of the Lord but also in the eyes of men. (2 Corinthians 8:21)

Finally, brothers, whatever is true, whatever is noble, whatever is right, whatever is pure, whatever is lovely, whatever is admirable—if anything is excellent or praiseworthy—think about such things. (Philippians 4:8)

Live such good lives among the pagans that, though they accuse you of doing wrong, they may see your good deeds and glorify God on the day he visits us. (1 Peter 2:12)

Deal honestly with your fellow man. Tell the truth. Keep your promises. Say what you mean; mean what you say. People in the world should be impressed with your honesty and uprightness. Wouldn't it be wonderful if the whole world were bathed in a fresh breeze of integrity?

What Are the Marks of Integrity?

A person of integrity doesn't blame others for his own shortcomings. He doesn't say, "Look what you made me do!" Remember this guy?

> He lost his job, he wrecked his car.
> But he took his troubles like a man
> And blamed them all on his wife!

The person of integrity accepts responsibility for his own decisions and actions.

A person of integrity holds to his convictions under all circumstances. He does not consider what others will think or what reward he might get or what punishment it will bring. Someone said, "Everyone has three faces: one he shows, one he thinks he shows, and the one he has."

"Everyone has three faces: one he shows, one he thinks he shows, and the one he has."

A man asked a woman if she would go to bed with him for a thousand dollars. After careful deliberation she told him that, yes, for a thousand dollars she would consent to have sex with him.

He said, "How about for a dollar?"

Sarcastically she spat out, "What kind of woman do you think I am?"

He replied, "We've already found that out. We're just haggling over the price."

Joyce Hifler wrote in her terrific column, that appears in syndicated newspapers, "Think on These Things,"

The Fresh Breeze of Integrity

Don't worry about who people think you are. Consider who you think you are. Be someone you can depend on. Be steadfast in good times and bad. Tell fear to get lost and resist doubt with all your heart. Laugh at yourself. Humor is a saving grace. But laughing at other people makes us fools instead of friends. Watch out for self-criticism. It is so easy to fall into the habit of seeing ourselves doing nothing right. Don't respond to critics' words. If a lesson exists learn it, but give yourself credit for knowing something. Fight the urge to fight. Don't argue with stupidity. It only makes us stupid. When you need a friend, be one to yourself and someone else. Like attracts like, nothing counts for nothing. Invest in beauty—that of the spirit that comes in love. It's yours for the taking.

Dale Wimbrow, wrote this marvelous little poem:

The Man in the Glass

When you get what you want in your struggle
    for self
    And the whole world makes you king for a day
Just go to a mirror and look at yourself,
    And see what *that* man has to say.

For it isn't your father or mother or wife
    Whose judgment upon you must pass;
The fellow whose verdict counts most in your
    life,
    Is the one staring back from the glass.

Some people may think you a straight-shooting
    chum
    And call you a wonderful guy,
But the man in the glass says you're only a bum
    If you can't look him straight in the eye.

He's the fellow to please, never mind all the rest,
For he's with you clear up to the end.
And you've passed your most dangerous, diffi-
cult test
If the man in the glass is your friend.

You may fool the whole world down the path-
way of life,
And get pats on your back as you pass.
But your final reward will be heartaches and tears,
If you've cheated the man in the glass.

A person of integrity values honor above cost. Arthur Gordon, author of *A Touch of Wonder,* tells of a famous surgeon working with a new nurse. She was worried about being adequate for such a well-known and respected man.

He said, "I'm ready to close. Did we get all twelve sponges out of the patient?"

The nurse nervously replied, "I only counted eleven."

"There were twelve. I'm going to go ahead and close."

The nurse felt panic. She was new. This doctor had done this procedure hundreds of times. She knew he knew what he was doing. But she stuck to her guns. "I only counted eleven!"

The doctor insisted, "I counted twelve. You're new at this. We're closing."

But the nurse blurted out, "I only counted eleven. We're not closing until I've seen that twelfth sponge."

The doctor moved his right shoe to the side, revealing the twelfth sponge. As she looked at the sponge, he smiled and said, "You'll do." That's integrity!

A person of integrity values right above reward. James Garfield was the twentieth president of the United States. He was assassinated in 1881. It is lesser known that he was an elder in his church and a Sunday school teacher. During his presidency a crisis arose and an emergency cabinet meeting was called for the following Sunday morning.

The Fresh Breeze of Integrity

The president respectfully declined to attend the meeting, saying that he had a previous appointment that took precedence over this one. The crisis passed. The nation survived.

The president was later asked, "Just what kind of appointment was more important than that cabinet meeting?"

Mr. Garfield replied, "That appointment, Sir, was with my Lord. I have faithfully attended worship every Sunday, and I intend to do so the rest of my life."

Henry Clay, a nineteenth-century orator and statesman, seemed almost certain to become America's next president, but he took the unpopular side of a very hot political question. A friend and advisor said, "Henry, if you continue to hold that stand you will never be president of the United States." Henry Clay stuck to his convictions. But his friend was right—he never became president. But these words that defined his exemplary life were carved on his tombstone: "I'd rather be right than president!"

That's the fresh breeze of integrity!

A person of integrity acts in the best interest of his fellowman. That's the real definition of love. No, love isn't "the feeling you feel when you feel you've got a feeling that you've never felt before." Love seeks the best for the object of that love.

If it doesn't serve others' interests, it isn't love. And it isn't right.

The mother of James and John came to Jesus. She wanted him to guarantee her two sons a special place of prominence in his kingdom. Jesus responded with a great lesson on humility and not trying to claw your way to the top, call the shots, or win through intimidation. He said if you really want to be great, you've got to serve others. He concluded by saying, "Whoever wants to be first must be

Love isn't "the feeling you feel when you feel you've got a feeling that you've never felt before."

your slave—just as the Son of Man did not come to be served, but to serve, and to give his life as a ransom for many" (Matthew 20:28). Integrity!

A person of integrity seeks the will of God in all things. Wasn't Gethsemane a marvelous lesson in integrity? As Jesus faced Calvary, he prayed alone in Gethsemane. He felt the burden of being the savior of the world. He faced the horrible pain the cross would bring. Who would really care? What difference would it make? So he prayed, "My Father, if it is possible, may this cup be taken from me. Yet not as I will, but as you will" (Matthew 26:39). He knew what was right. It was *right* to do the Father's will. It was *right* to die for those he loved. It was *not* possible to be who he was or do what he came to do and escape the cross. "Yet not as I will, but as *you* will."

The disciples picked up on this concept. Jesus met Peter while he was fishing. Jesus said, "Throw out your nets, and you will catch some fish."

I love Peter's answer: "Master, we've worked hard all night and haven't caught anything. But *because you say so,* I will let down the nets" (Luke 5:5).

Just look at what Peter was saying: "Lord, we are fishermen. We know what we're doing. And we've been doing it all night. The fish just aren't biting." Here's the part that's good: "But *because you say so,* I will let down the nets." That's acknowledging the sovereignty of God. That's submission to God because he is God. That's integrity! And because Peter submitted they caught so many fish the nets began to break. God blesses obedience. He loves integrity.

Everyone knows the beloved apostle Paul. He first believed Jesus was a fake. He persecuted Christians. He gained authority to go to Damascus to do more of the same, but on that road he met up with Jesus. Convinced Jesus really was the Son of God, the promised Messiah, he asked Jesus, "Lord, what do you want me to do?" (Acts 9:5). No cop out. No rationalization. No seeking to escape the facts. Rather, he acted on the facts, and his humble response led to one of the most exemplary and effective lives ever lived in the service of Jesus Christ.

The world could use an epidemic of integrity. How about letting it start with you and me? We might start a breeze that would turn into a whirlwind!

Happiness is an inside job. It's more of a choice than a set of circumstances. Many people miss out on happiness because they think, "I could be happy *if only....* " I'm convinced that happiness is possible for anyone, no matter the circumstances.

Some people confuse aloneness with loneliness, but they are not the same thing. Make no mistake, many people are both alone *and* lonely. Others, even though surrounded by family, friends, and associates, are lonely nonetheless. The catch is to learn how to be alone without being lonely.

Some singles have trouble with this. They talk of their aloneness as "four walls crushing in on me" or "deafening silence." They say, "I long to be held and touched," or "I'd give anything to hear another human voice."

One single lady had had her fill of these woe-is-me, pity-party letters to a noted newspaper columnist. She thought the other side of the coin should be heard. In effect she said, "I am forty-two, never married, and manager of customer relations at a large city bank. I'm happy with my house. It's where I can escape and be myself. I've got pets. I'm not frightened, bored, or lonely. My life is full. It just doesn't include a husband and kids. I have dozens of nieces and nephews when I want to be around children. I have time to read, cook for my friends, watch *what* I want to on TV *when* I want to watch it. I go to art classes, concerts, and museums. I love my job, and I'll be president of the company someday. I'm tired of reading about frightened, lonely women who are working just until they can find a man to take care of them. I'm tired of hearing how awful it is being single."

We All Have Lots of Alone Time

We thank this dear lady for reminding us that loneliness is not inevitably linked with aloneness. It's not a matter of being single or being married. She wants us to quit stereotyping single women as miserable, terrified, husband-hunting, bitter, deprived nymphomaniacs. It's time happy singles got equal time.

Everyone is alone sometimes—whether for short periods of time or long. People are alone before marriage, and people are sometimes alone after marriage. For some couples, separation is brought about by problems in the marriage, for others separation is brought on by military duty overseas or extended business trips. And of course, some are divorced or widowed. Even when people wake up in the middle of the night or get up early in the morning before their mate awakens, they are somewhat alone.

Inner peace and poise and serenity can be ours whether married or single. Such peace allows us to accept the *now* circumstances without feeling locked in or crushed. Being alone can be a time of blooming, not wilting; it can be a cherished time, not a dreaded time.

Whether or Not You're Lonely Isn't Determined by Marital Status

Some singles feel they must marry to be happy; they feel incomplete without a marriage partner. The apostle Paul was one of the greatest characters in the Bible. He was single. And he wrote about it in these words:

> It is good for a man not to marry. But since there is so much immorality, each man should have his own wife, and each woman her own husband. . . . I wish that all men were as I am [single]. But each man has his own gift from God; one has this gift, another has that. (1 Corinthians 7:1–2, 7)

Now to be sure, there was a special circumstance surrounding Paul's advice—Christians were being persecuted. Paul felt a single man could handle persecution better than a man who had the concern for a wife and family. Be that as it may, Paul chose to be single, and he placed his stamp of approval on anyone else who chose the same route.

Remember too, that the greatest man who ever lived was single—Jesus Christ. He certainly could have married. No doubt many women would have welcomed the chance to be the wife of Jesus. But because of his mission, he chose to spend his entire thirty-three years as a single person. He was alone, but he certainly wasn't lonely. We simply must learn

Being alone can be a time of blooming, not wilting; it can be a cherished time, not a dreaded time.

that inner peace is not a matter of being married or single. Marrieds or singles can be alone without being lonely.

Marriage does not necessarily rule out loneliness. It's true that it has worked out wonderfully well for some. It could and should for all. My mom was twice blessed. She was married to my dad for thirty-nine years. A couple of years after his death, she married another wonderful Christian man. I had the honor of doing their marriage ceremony. They had another twenty-one years of happiness. My dad and mom were close. My mom and my stepdad were also very loving, affectionate, and close. But it must also be said that some of the most miserable, lonely people in the world are married. Some marriages have turned dreams into nightmares.

Rules That Rule Out Loneliness

Be comfortable with who you are. "Because of the present crisis, I think that it is good for you to remain as you are. Are you married? Do not seek a divorce. Are you unmarried? Do not look for a wife" (1 Corinthians 7:26–27).

It must be said again that these were unusual times. The church was facing major hardship. But the point is that you need to be satisfied in your present circumstances—whatever they are. Here are further words from Paul:

> I have learned to be content whatever the circumstances. I know what it is to be in need, and I know what it is to have plenty. I have learned the secret of being content in any and every situation, whether well fed or hungry, whether living in plenty or in want. I can do everything through him who gives me strength. (Philippians 4:11–13)

If you can't change it, don't sweat it. Accept your circumstances. Bloom where you are planted.

Alone but Not Lonely

Make positive affirmations. What you tell yourself affects who you are. We become what we prophesy about ourselves. We tend to magnify all the negative things we see in ourselves and downplay all the good. Why we do this, I don't know. But I know we have choice about it. A good place to practice positive affirmation is in front of your bathroom mirror. Say things that are true, and *choose* to believe them. There are three such affirmations I use in my Peak of the Week class every Wednesday night. I have the audience stand and repeat these statements after me at the top of their voices:

- I'm made in God's image!
- I can choose my attitude!
- I choose to feel great!

Try these tomorrow morning. Look yourself in the eye. Say them with feeling. Laugh a little, but *believe* you are telling the truth. Do this for twenty-one days in a row, and I guarantee you'll believe what you're saying. More importantly, you'll act out the positive image you're projecting.

Here are a couple of others:

- Today I will not put myself down, and I will not allow anyone else to put me down.

- Today I will allow myself to be happy, and I will *choose* to be happy.

Give this the twenty-one-day test. You'll be amazed at the results.

Develop an awareness of the world around you. God has created a marvelous world; take in the beauty of his creation. I wrote part of this book while in Alaska. I was doing a family camp at Camp Challenge near a beautiful little town called Wasilla. Early Sunday morning I sat down on the dock and looked out over the lake. No one else was there. The lake was like a mirror, reflecting the lovely mountains in the background. The only sounds were the magnificent call of the loons and the splash of salmon jumping out of the water and back to their habitat. It was peaceful and still. All seemed right with the world.

What's nice is that you don't have to go to Alaska or Hawaii or some other exotic place to find peace. There are sunsets where you live. The birds sing, and the flowers bloom. Be aware that you live in a wonderful world. It's also filled with lovely people. Sometimes you just have to stop and focus. Lonely people allow their problems to blind them to this canopy of beauty. It's all yours for the looking. Take it in!

The best defense is a good offense. You hear that defense wins games. I wouldn't doubt it for the world. But the truth is, if your team scores everytime it gets the ball, you'll win the game. I was in the Korean conflict. There were all kinds of ways to get into trouble over there. GIs had lots of time on their hands and not many ways to spend their money. Gambling, drinking, and women were all available for a very small price. It wasn't the fault of the Korean people. War just does that to a country. They told us that if we would stay busy doing good stuff, we would be able to resist the temptations.

I found this to be true. I read my Bible more. I researched subjects and wrote articles on various themes. I helped start a church in a flight-line chapel that pilots used before they went out on their missions. I took a night job in the officers' club to make a few extra dollars to send home. It worked for me. I got home with my health, honor, morals, and spirituality intact.

Happy people are busy people. That was the key for the lady at the beginning of this chapter. She was simply too busy doing good, exciting, and rewarding things to be lonely.

This is also true in the church. There are the *lifters* and the *leaners*. Some people are part of the solution, and others are only part of the problem. The old mule can't kick while he's pulling, and he can't pull while he's kicking. You've got to take an active, involved role to be a happy Christian.

Take a genuine interest in people. Don't be afraid to love people. It's true that you may get burned, but the alternative is fearful.

When fear shuts out love, you shrivel up inside and die. Love is vulnerable. If you can't bleed, you can't bloom. You've got to take a chance on love. Some people love things and use people. Successful people love people and use things. Put yourself in the middle of people—good people, interesting people. Mix with them. Highly esteem them. Cooperating with people in good projects is a positive guarantee against loneliness.

Secure the companionship of the Lord. David, in his marvelous twenty-third Psalm said, "Even though I walk through the valley of the shadow of death, I will fear no evil, for you are with me; your rod and your staff, they comfort me" (v. 4). And listen to Paul: "I can do everything through him who gives me strength" (Philippians 4:13). And Jesus said, "Never will I leave you; never will I forsake you" (Hebrews 13:5).

Christians are never alone, never without someone who cares.

You can learn the secret. You will often be alone, but you never need to be lonely. It's really a choice that anyone can make; it's a skill that anyone can learn—being alone, but not lonely.

> Love is vulnerable. If you can't bleed, you can't bloom.

Chapter Twenty-One

Don't Let Me Die 'Til I'm Dead

The title of this chapter actually came from Cavett Robert, the founding father of the National Speaker's Association. It's been my privilege to know this great man and to appear on the speaking platform with him on several occasions. Cavett has a gesture for every syllable. He retired from his law practice in New York and was sent to Arizona with a life expectancy of less than six months. He's lived years beyond that and continues to thrill audiences with his wit and charm. Somewhere in his speech you'll see him half bent over, arms outstretched, saying, "Lord, don't let me die 'til I'm dead!"

There's a lot more to living than breathing. We see some poor soul lying in a hospital in a coma. We say, "He's just a vegetable." Others are in nursing homes sitting in wheel chairs with blank stares on their faces. Nobody comes to see them. Their quality of life has gone.

Then there are the physically healthy dead. They're the ones we speak of in this chapter. Their blood pressure may be normal, their heart rate may be terrific, they are not necessarily overweight or suffering from some terminal illness, but they've lost the wonder of life. They have no vitality of life or appetite for living. Loving, laughing, and learning is a thing of the past. The Bible speaks of a woman living in sin and says she is "dead even while she lives" (1 Timothy 5:6). Life was not meant to be boring or an endless chain of empty cycles. Here are a few more "Lord don't let mes" . . .

Lord, Don't Let Me Die with My Music Still in Me

There's a lot of living to do—places to visit, things to do, contributions to make. There's joy in creativity and spontaneity. Without this joy, life would make no sense. Someone said,

> We all make footprints in the sands of time;
> For some, the mark of a great soul.
> For others, only the mark of a heel.

No one can take your place. You might as well be you. No one else is qualified for the job.

There is wonderful potential in every human life. Some people's potential is the arts. Just think how many great songs have been composed and sung. There are just as many yet to be created. You may have one or more of these bursting in your soul. Or you may hold great paintings, sculpture, poetry, and plays inside you, just waiting to be expressed—let them out!

Others may be gifted in communication, leadership, compassion, or organization. The Bible says *all* of us have been given great gifts from God. He expects us to use these to better the world in which we live and to lead men to Jesus. Listen to Paul:

> We have different gifts, according to the grace given us. If a man's gift is prophesying, let him use it in proportion to his faith. If it is serving, let him serve; if it is teaching, let him teach; if it is encouraging, let him encourage; if it is contributing to the needs of others, let him give generously; if it is leadership, let him govern diligently; if it is showing mercy, let him do it cheerfully. (Romans 12:6–8)

How do we die with our music still in us? Normally, it's when you die prematurely. Perhaps it's an awful automobile crash that takes the life of a twenty-six-year-old man or a terrible disease that claims the young mother of thirty-five. Birth and death dates on tombstones subtract out to every possible age. You're a good dying age. One miss of the heart, and they're sticking a lily in your hand and lowering the top on your knotty-pine convertible.

Others die emotionally and spiritually while their bodies live on. They let their gifts lie dormant. They have closed their eyes to beauty and challenge. As an old song says, "No one wants to be old at thirty-three"—but many are.

> No one can take your place. You might as well be you. No one else is qualified for the job.

Don't Let Me Outlive My Zest for Life

The difference between delightful old people and crotchety old people is often zest for life. I was doing the funeral for my wife's brother, and "Old John," the ninety-year-old brother-in-law to the widow, was there. His hearing was practically gone, but he joined in animated conversation and was very helpful in handling many of the details associated with the death. He knew all about forms that had to be filled out—where to get them and how to get them filed. He was delightfully alive.

Tulsa fitness guru, Floyd Hall, eighty-nine, wrote a book on how to do away with back pain. He called it *Healthwise Exercise before You Rise.* On Mother's Day, Sarah Saklad, ninety-seven, of Lowell, Massachusetts, received her high school diploma. She was valedictorian of her class, which was made up of nursing home residents! Contrast these with careful old people who won't even buy green bananas.

Don't Let the Flowers Come Too Late

Everyone has a right to love, praise, and recognition, but you can't force people to give them to you. In order to receive these blessings, you've got to spread lots of them around. They have a way of coming back to you: "Give, and it will be given to you. A good measure, pressed down, shaken together and running over, will be poured into your lap. For with the measure you use, it will be measured to you" (Luke 6:38).

Marriage is one place you need to lay on plenty of flowers:

Tell Her So

Amid the cares of married strife,
In spite of toil and business life,
If you value your dear wife,
    Tell her so!

There was a time you thought it bliss
To get the favor of a kiss.

Don't Let Me Die 'Til I'm Dead

A dozen now, won't come amiss.
>   Tell her so!

Don't act as if she's past her prime,
As tho' to please her were a crime,
If ever you loved her, now's the time.
>   Tell her so!

Never let her heart grow cold,
Richer beauties will unfold.
She is worth her weight in gold,
>   Tell her so!

You are hers and hers alone;
Well you know she's all your own;
Don't wait to carve it on a stone,
>   Tell her so!

>   Anonymous

A husband once asked, "When's the best time to tell your wife you love her?" The answer came back quickly, "Before someone else does!" It reminds me of the fellow who didn't kiss his wife for twenty years and then shot the man who did!

Don't Let Me Believe My Fan Mail

Everyone in the limelight gets love/hate mail. Fan mail is a blessing; it can also be a curse. Hate mail comes with the limelight too. If you believe either kind too much, you'll be in trouble. That's what may have happened to Jim and Tammy Bakker or to Gary Hart. Eventually, others may see you as larger-than-life. When you begin seeing yourself that way, look out!

Herod was a cheap politician. The people of Tyre and Sidon sought audience with him to make peace. Herod decided to strut his stuff before these people. He put on his dazzling silver robe and stood before them in the bright noonday sun to make a speech. The people shouted, "This is the voice of a god not a man!"

Herod said to himself, "I think they have something here." And because he "gave not God the glory," he was struck down and eaten by worms, and he died! (See Acts 12:19–23.)

Hopefully, you'll get enough praise to keep you motivated. I know you'll get enough criticism to keep you humble.

Don't Let the Turkeys Get You Down

A friend of mine gave me a card that read, "You become what you eat." And of course this was said as I was biting into my turkey sandwich. You've heard it's hard to soar with the eagles in the morning if you've run with the turkeys the night before. And there are plenty of turkeys around! They're the people who spout negative thinking.

It's hard to soar with the eagles in the morning if you've run with the turkeys the night before.

They know all the reasons it *can't* be done. They are full of criticism. You can't do anything right in the eyes of a turkey. And enough *digs* make a grave. The cemeteries are full of preachers the brethren have killed. Too often in the church we kill our dreamers and shoot our wounded. In every arena of life, those out front trying to do something are often the targets of the turkeys behind them.

Anyone doing anything worthwhile will be shot at by those who sincerely disagree, by those jealous of their accomplishments, and by those who just want to cover the tracks of their own inactivity. Be strong enough to ask, "Is the criticism valid?" Then ask, "What can I do to improve?" But keep on doing what you believe in doing with all your heart.

Don't Let Me Stay, When I Should Go Home

I'm glad that society is becoming better informed on the limitations of life-support devices. Sometimes doctors hold on to their patients with machinery after quality of life is gone. Sometimes loved ones just can't give up, so they keep their loved one breathing, but comatose, long after quality of life is over.

I think of a couple in Texas who were among our dearest friends. Cancer invaded the body of the man. It ravaged his body. Deterioration was fast. Life-support systems were suggested, but not accepted. Instead, she held her beloved husband in her arms, whispered sweet words of love in his ear, and told him it was time for him to go home. She gave him permission to go. Within minutes he sighed deeply and went home to the Lord.

We're not going to be here forever. We've got somewhere else to go. Most of us fear dying too soon or living too long. I've decided how I want my funeral conducted. I want it in the Garnett Church of Christ in Tulsa, Oklahoma. That church has been my life since 1970. It's the center of my ministry and mission. I want songs of faith and celebration. I want the service ended there. Let the hearse and casket go to the cemetery. Let the people stay at the church building. Let them love and minister to one another and leave to complete their own preparation for the trip home. I love living! And I know it's going to be fantastic going home.

So, Lord, let me squeeze every drop out of life. Let me run the race with joy. And *don't let me die 'til I'm dead!*

Chapter Twenty-Two

You're Only as Rich as Your Relationships

Once there was a prosperous business man. He wore the best clothes and ate the best meals. He did without nothing. There was a guy lying at his gate—just a tramp, a hobo—and all he wanted was the leftovers from one of those fabulous meals. Dogs came and licked the tramp's sores, but the rich man did nothing for him.

As time went by both men died. It's strange, but the story only mentions the funeral of the rich man. All it says about the beggar's death is, "The beggar died also." But then something phenomenal happened! The beggar was carried by angels to Abraham's side. The rich man died and lifted up his eyes in torment. It's ironic that such opposites could completely change positions at death. The rich man was sorry for his neglect of his fellowman. He asked for a second chance. But he was told that after death there is no second chance. You've got to get it right the first time.

We tend to judge riches by material prosperity. We measure success by visible things such as health, wealth, and position.

This Bible story shows us a man whom the world would declare a tremendous success. In truth, he was a terrible failure.

Who Really Is Successful?

How do we measure success? What is the standard of prosperity?

If money is the measuring stick, how much money is required? Does it follow that the more you have the more successful you are? People must think so, because they go to great lengths to accumulate status symbols—rich folks' toys.

After death there is no second chance. You've got to get it right the first time.

Is position the measure of success? If you are president of your firm or the chief executive officer, does that make you successful? Is it titles? Is it the fact that you were *elected?* Is it education or beauty? Is it athletic prowess? There are many really successful people in our world today who have no money, position, or any of the other things listed here. What is loud and clear is that these material things are not a proper measure of a person's success or prosperity.

Relationships Are the Only True Measure of Riches

Good relationships are essential to success and true riches. Money can't buy the love of a good woman. It can't secure friendship, loyalty, or trust. Nothing can substitute for good relationships. Relationships are the final determiner of life's worth.

So, Americans spend most of their time, talent, and treasures trying to cultivate good relationships, right? Wrong! We're in hot pursuit of higher paying jobs. Never mind the hours or the stress. Money is the thing; the paycheck more than compensates, we tell ourselves. We end up working overtime or moonlighting a second job. We make a lot more money, yes. But riches, *no!* Often our happiness goes out the same window the rush for more money came in.

We neglect the only true measure of success. If the car breaks down, we rush it to the mechanic and pay whatever it takes to fix it. If my golf ball is slicing off to the right and landing in a sand trap, I spend big bucks on a golf professional to help me correct my swing. But if a relationship is suffering, we often do absolutely nothing about it. It's like those two guys who claimed to be bosom buddies. "There's nothing we wouldn't do for each other. And that's exactly what we've been doing for each other these past years—nothing!"

> Nothing can substitute for good relationships. Relationships are the final determiner of life's worth.

Four Relationships That Measure Your Success

First, there's the relationship you have with yourself—with who you are in the present, with what you've been in the past, and with what you can be in the future. When looking at your present self, don't brag about your color, sex, or nationality. You had absolutely nothing to do with any of them. Don't waste time wishing you were someone else. Accept yourself. That's the key to confidence, maturity, and success.

Then there's your relationship with your past—what you've done and where you've been. The difference between the apostles Peter and Judas was how they dealt with their pasts. Which sin was worse—Judas's betrayal of Jesus or Peter's denial that he even knew him.

Judas was filled with remorse and went out and hanged himself. The sad thing about suicide is that you don't have a chance to undo it and learn from past mistakes. Suicide has been defined as the worse form of self-criticism.

Peter was also filled with remorse over denying the Lord. He went out and wept bitterly, but he came back to the Master's side. It was Peter who preached the first gospel sermon on Pentecost morning. Peter took the gospel to the Gentiles for the first time. Peter is the principal character in the first half of the book of Acts and the author of the epistles First and Second Peter. You've got to come to grips with your past. It's not so much what has happened to you as what you do about what has happened to you that matters.

You also need to come to grips with your future. Believe in the outcome. Be positive about where you are heading. I love what the flight attendant always says as we begin our landing here at home: "Have a pleasant day in Tulsa *or wherever your final destination may be.*" It's nice to know that Tulsa is not my final destination. It's just a stopping off place on my way to heaven.

Secondly, there's the relationship with your family. Have you given it proper priority on your agenda? Pour large doses of love, acceptance, and forgiveness on your spouse, kids, and parents. Don't let any material thing become more important to you than a rich and rewarding relationship with your family. Life is too short to sweat the small stuff. Don't get so involved with making a living that you don't make a life.

Thirdly, there's the relationship you have with other people. Cultivate at least seven friends during your life. You're going to need them when you die—six to carry you, and one to preach! Jess Lair, author of *I Ain't Much, Baby, But I'm All I've Got!* talks about his five friends. These, he says, are the kind of friendships you spent time, effort, and money on. These friends are the kind you can call in the middle of the night and know they'll come running. They'd give you the shirts off their backs. And you'd give them yours. To have friends like that, you've got to be a friend like that. Be the kind of person other folks want for a friend.

The relationship you have with business associates is also important. The Bible says, "If it is possible, as far as it depends on you, live at peace with everyone" (Romans 12:18). Give out large amounts of courtesy and fairness. Go the second mile. Value everyone as human beings created in the image of God.

You also have a relationship with the world around you. Maybe you don't think you need other people. Just try doing business without them. Remember the golden rule—and it's *not* "He who has the gold . . . rules," it's "Do to others as you would have them do to you" (Luke 6:31).

Fourthly, there is your relationship with God. Back to the story at the beginning of this chapter. The rich man did great in business. The world looked up to him. Mothers pointed their

> Don't get so involved with making a living that you don't make a life.

sons to him as an example. And he had everything . . . everything, that is, except what he needed most. He had no relationship with God. "This is how it will be with anyone who stores up things for himself but is not rich toward God."

Hundreds of thousands of people lined the streets of Dallas that day. All eyes were on that impressive young man riding in the convertible. Rich. Powerful. Most prestigious job in America. Riding by his side was his beautiful wife. No doubt many in the crowd that day thought, "Man, I'd give anything in the world to trade places with that guy." And then a shot rang out from the Texas School Book Depository building, and the only thing that mattered was how things stood between John Fitzgerald Kennedy and God.

If you're successful with these four relationships, you are rich, no matter what else you may not have. If you don't have them, you are poor, no matter what else you may possess. And the good news is, there is still time to build these four relationships in your life. So get going!

Chapter
Twenty-Three

America
the
Beautiful

It's March 6, 1991. Never has America watched so much TV as in the past two months. Never have so many experts paraded before us on international television—military, political, and economic experts. We've come through seven weeks of air war and one hundred hours of ground war. We've suffered less than a hundred casualties. We've probably killed over a hundred thousand of the enemy while at war with one of the worst world tyrants ever. General Thomas Kelly said of Iraq, "The fourth largest army in the world has been reduced to the second largest army in its own nation." The media told us more than we ever wanted to know about what went on. The Iraqi press told its people lies of victory, saying Americans were defecting in droves and dying like flies.

America Has Been at War Before

We've had historic wars against England, France, and Spain. Wars were fought for our independence and freedom. We suffered the horrible Civil War (what a misnomer) of the 1860s. Then came World Wars I and II. Patriotism was at its highest. Our servicemen and -women were honored, respected, and celebrated. Those who fell in combat were mourned and martyred. Those who returned were welcomed with ticker tape parades and meetings with the president.

Then came Korea and Vietnam and the loss of American credibility and unity—especially with Vietnam. There were stories of drugs, dishonor, and division. There was unrest at home and riots on campuses. The bright gleem of the stars and stripes dimmed in world vision. The small nation of Iran held American hostages for 454 days while America and the world looked on helplessly. Was America, after all, just a paper tiger?

Turnaround

Then came August 1990. Iraq made its infamous invasion of Kuwait. A helpless little country was brutalized, terrorized, and vandalized. Kuwait was robbed, raped, and pillaged. Many Americans thought it was about oil. They protested sending American troops to the rescue. "No blood for oil," they shouted. President George Bush stood firm. America rallied behind its leader. The United Nations made resolutions and told the criminal nation, "You have until January 15 to get out." It was the national *Gunfight at the OK Corral.* Gary Cooper was back in *High Noon!* Matt Dillon was meeting Black Bart in the street in front on the Long Branch, and John Wayne was sporting his green beret again.

But this was no television show. Real bullets were being fired. Real bombs were being dropped, this time with high-tech precision like the world had never seen before. Bombs from an airplane several thousand feet in the sky could slide along a lazer beam right down the stairs into the basement of a predetermined target. Real planes were being shot down. Real scud missiles were plowing into American barracks. And real Americans and buddies from coalition forces were being killed.

Victory came in less than fifty days. Saddam Hussein was brought to his knees (at least temporarily). After fighting the Americans, he began a fight for his own survival in his own country.

Patriotism Again at an All-Time High

The war was tragic and senseless, as all wars are, but it worked wonders for patriotism in America. Yellow ribbons were worn and displayed everywhere. You saw them on car radio antennas. People wore them on badges and pins on their clothing. Flags were flown on thousands of houses and buildings. The popularity of President Bush went through the roof. Never has a president enjoyed more support from his people.

America was gearing up to welcome home its heroes. A Cleveland, Oklahoma, marine pilot who had been shot down over Iraq was listed as missing in action. But when he was finally found, rescued, and returned home, kids from the local high school marched to his home in celebration of his safe return.

Many new songs were written. America geared up for parades and celebrations "when Johnny comes marching home again."

"I'm Proud to Be an American"

Lee Greenwood's ever popular song, "I'm Proud to Be an American" gained new popularity. General Norman Schwarzkopf fanned its flame by playing it for his troops

America is just a teenager with pimples—puberty with a promise.

every morning. America is indeed the "land of the free and the home of the brave." What a history we have—from pilgrims escaping to the New World for religious freedom to war protesters across the street from the White House. This is a unique and beautiful land.

You've noticed America has no "out-igration" quota. You can leave any time and go anywhere. You are equally free to stay. You can fight for your rights and freedom. You can pitch in and improve. You can participate in every just cause and maybe even be elected to political office. Ask any immigrant who has been here any length of time.

America is not over the hill. It's just a baby. Egypt has pyramids, the oldest man-made structures in the world. England, France, Ireland, and Scotland have castles from the fifteenth century. In America, when a building is just one hundred years old, it's "condemned!" Whatever is wrong with America is not senility; it's only acne. America is just a teenager with pimples—puberty with a promise.

America is the best friend the world has ever had. Ask the people of South Korea, South Vietnam, Granada, Kuwait, and Saudi Arabia. Ask the people of Bosnia. Go wherever floods, earthquakes, tornadoes, war, and famine have been. America could stay out of a lot of trouble if it would just mind its own business and turn a blind eye to the hurts of fellow human beings in distant lands. But Americans can't do that. Helping others defines us. It's what being an American is all about!

Take Another Look at America

Freedom! Freedom of speech and worship. Freedom of the press. Freedom from want. Americans are free to travel anywhere in the land without having to obtain a permit and pass through check points.

We haven't licked prejudice yet, but we're working on it. There are more black millionaires in America than anywhere else in the world. General Colin Powell led our armed forces as Chief of Staff, and a large number of people wanted to see him become America's first black president. Any person in America has the opportunity to become anything he or she wants to become.

What Do We Do about America?

Let's don't gloss over America's imperfections, but don't ignore her blessings either. Be proud of her glorious heritage. Celebrate her heroes. Work for solutions to her problems. Enjoy her resources. Love her people. America is still "one nation under God." Honor her God. Pray for her future. God bless America!

Chapter Twenty-Four

The Operation Was a Success but the Patient Died

I knew it was coming. And I know it must be true. I read it in the *Nashville Banner.* It was an article about new technology in foods.

Gene splicing may soon produce lettuce that fights disease! Peaches are coming that don't grow on trees. And the crowning accomplishment of the decade? We could soon be eating chocolate cake that has no calories. The article further speculated that eventually science will be able to produce almost any food we like, but with zero calories. It's the ultimate anorectic food. You eat it, you feel satisfied, and you starve to death with a smile on your face.

A guy was in an automobile accident. He woke up at the scene but then fainted dead away. This happened a couple of times. Finally the guy standing in front of the victim moved away, revealing the "S" on the SHELL sign. The next time the poor man woke up, he was greatly relieved.

A lady was in the hospital for major surgery. As she woke up in her room, she happened to glance out her window. There was a terrible fire next door. She thought the operation had failed.

I like the one about the lady wanting to make contact with her late husband, Ernie. The spiritualist got into a deep trance. Finally a voice came from a long way off: "Margaret, send me some cigarettes." Then the voice faded into silence.

"Wait," said Margaret, "he didn't say where to send them."

The spiritualist replied, "You notice he didn't ask for matches."

Can you stand one more spiritualist joke? Charlie visited a spiritualist. During the trance the spiritualist began laughing hysterically. Finally in desperation, Charlie slapped her in the face. They put him in jail. You guessed it, the charge was "striking a happy medium."

Opportunity still abounds in America. The free enterprise system is alive and doing well. Entreprenuerism is thriving. But many opt for con games or get-rich-quick schemes that bring immediate, but temporary success. The money comes in and the good life is experienced briefly, but there is cause and effect to reckon with. Man must live with the consequences of his decisions. The piper must be paid. There *ain't* no free lunch. It's payday, someday. "Crime does not pay" is an old, but true adage. The Bible says "Be sure your sins will find you out" (Numbers 32:23). The operation was a success but the patient died.

The High Cost of Low Living

Immorality promises much but delivers little. Many young people experiment with premarital sex only to suffer unwanted pregnancy or sexually transmitted diseases. Extramarital affairs entice many. "She's everything I've ever wanted" follows "she doesn't understand me." Moments, or even years, of illicit pleasure eventually reap exposure, divorce, and loss of reputation and soul.

There are those who don't want the commitment that marriage demands. Divorce becomes an easy alternative. They jump from bed to bed or visit a psychiatrist who tells them the problem is that they feel guilty. So they stop feeling guilty, while continuing the lifestyle. But that lifestyle doesn't make them happy now. And there is God to face in the judgment.

Remember the game Russian Roulette? You take a six-shooter revolver, insert one bullet, spin the chamber, put the gun to your temple, and pull the trigger. The chances are five to one that nothing will happen. But that one chance is fatal! You'd be a fool to play this game, but many do.

Many, who would never think of playing Russian Roulette with a gun, do it all the time with their lives. "Just this once" ends up with virginity gone and a whole new set of problems. "Just this once" is a drink that becomes drunkenness, loss of control, an accident, and death.

A drinker never *intends* to become an alcoholic. A passionate teenager who loses control never *wants* to get pregnant. That first marijuana cigarette is not *supposed* to make you an addict. The man who breaks into his first house never *meant* to become a lifetime thief. The prospects look good. You think you'll get a little pleasure, a little satisfaction, and good things will come into your life. But hear the voice of Scripture: "But each one is tempted when, by his own evil desire, he is dragged away and enticed. Then, after desire has conceived, it gives birth to sin; and sin, when it is full-grown, gives birth to death. Don't be deceived, my dear brothers" (James 1:14–16).

Living as Though Christ Never Died

"I don't go to church anymore." That's what she said. She got tired of all the effort. Now she doesn't have to do what Christians have to do. She doesn't have to go to church, never reads her Bible, and doesn't have to give of her time, talent, or money. It's a big relief.

I spoke at a funeral today. John Morris was fifty-three. He and his wife were sitting on the couch watching television when he just sighed and fell over into his wife's lap. He died instantly. John was a Christian. He was nineteen when he married Betty and she was sixteen. They were charter members of the church I've served for over twenty-five years. They brought up their kids there. John was the first driver when we started our bus ministry to bring neighborhood kids to Sunday school. He was faithful to Jesus all his life. I don't know how much money he made. But when he died, the only thing that mattered was how things stood between John Morris and God. John was a success. Others make millions and live in the lap of luxury. They jet all over the world, have exotic friends, and do exotic things. But if you live as though Christ never died, you'll have to die as though Christ never lived.

> If you live as though Christ never died, you'll have to die as though Christ never lived.

Chapter Twenty-Five

The Party

The fifteenth chapter of Luke is my favorite chapter in the Bible. People misunderstood Jesus. They misunderstood church. Luke 15 is Jesus' attempt to set the record straight, to make it clear once and for all.

The Pharisees and teachers of the law were unhappy. They couldn't understand why Jesus permitted the tax collectors and sinners to be in the same crowd with them. Jesus was dismayed by their arrogance and prejudice. How could he make them realize they were *all* sinners? They all needed saving, and Jesus loved them all and wanted them all saved. So, to explain, Jesus told them four stories.

The Lost Sheep

Many of the listeners were shepherds. Those who weren't certainly knew about them. What if a shepherd loses one of his one hundred sheep? Wouldn't he leave the ninety-nine sheep safe in the fold and go out and search for the one that was lost? How well they knew he would. How many nights did a shepherd count his sheep and discover that one was missing? It was usually the same, stupid sheep. But he left the ninety-nine safely in the fold and went out to search for the one that was lost. It was only one, but he valued it that much. He simply searched until he found it. And when he found it, he didn't kick it all the way home. He put it on his shoulders and carried it home with rejoicing. He called in his neighbors. They had a party to celebrate finding that one lost sheep. And then Jesus delivered the punch line: "I tell you that in the same way there will be more rejoicing in heaven over one sinner who repents than over ninety-nine righteous persons who do not need to repent" (Luke 15:7).

The Lost Coin

The second story involved a woman who had ten coins and lost one. She lit a candle and swept the whole house in an effort to find the coin that was lost. This indicated a long search into the night. But her persistence paid off. She found the coin. She threw a party to celebrate and invited all the neighbors in. Again, the punch line: "In the same way, I tell you, there is rejoicing in the presence of the angels of God over one sinner who repents" (Luke 15:10).

A Runaway Boy

Story number three involved a runaway boy. A certain father had two sons. The younger of the two came to his dad. "Dad," he said, "Just give me what's coming to me.

The Party

I want your riches but not your rules. I'm hitting the road to find fame and fortune."

Sadly the father gave him his share of the estate. He packed his clothes and hit the road. He could hardly wait. He knew it was exciting out there. He had plenty of money in his pockets, and he was looking forward to a great time. And he *did* have a great time. A guy with money in his pockets always has friends around him. After all, he was buying the drinks and picking up the check. But the money ran out. A depression hit and the friends left. He had no where to go, and no one gave him anything. He searched the want ads. Finally he landed a job feeding pigs—a lowly job for a lost Jewish boy.

Christiani-ty is not so much "be good" or "do good." It is "come home!"

He was ripe for suicide or salvation. But the pigpen was his wake-up call. He came to his senses and figured out that the servants back home did better than he was doing. He made the greatest decision of his life: "'I will set out and go back to my father and say to him: Father, I have sinned against heaven and against you. I am no longer worthy to be called your son; make me like one of your hired men.' So he got up and went to his father" (Luke 15:18–19).

Verse 20 gets my vote as the most beautiful verse in the Bible: "But while he was a long way off, his father saw him and was filled with compassion for him; he ran to his son, threw his arms around him and kissed him."

What a reception wretched sinners get when they come home to Jesus. Christianity is not so much "be good" or "do good." It is "come home!"

And then came the party:

> The father said to his servants, "Quick! Bring the best robe and put it on him. Put a ring on his finger and sandals on his feet. Bring the fattened calf and kill it. Let's have a feast and celebrate.

For this son of mine was dead and is alive again; he was lost and is found." So they began to celebrate. (Luke 15:22–24)

A Boy at Home, but Also Lost

We must come back to these last verses. But for now, let's look at Jesus' fourth story (Luke 15:25–32). This boy's older brother was in the field. He heard the music and dancing. He asked a servant what was going on. They told him his brother had returned and that his father had thrown a party in his honor. The older brother puffed up like a Texas toad frog. He became angry and jealous.

"Father never threw a party like that for me," he probably thought. "And I've been out here slaving while my brother was tomcatting all over the country." And he would not go in to the party.

Here's the interesting thing. When he didn't come in, his father came looking for him. You see, the Father wants all his kids at the party. He urged his older son to come join in the fun.

The son repeated his allegation: "You never did anything like that for me!"

The father's reply is classic. "My son, you are always with me, and everything I have is yours. But we had to celebrate and be glad, because this brother of yours was dead and is alive again; he was lost and is found" (Luke 15:31–32).

Without a personal relationship with Jesus Christ, church is a drag.

Church Is a Party

Without a personal relationship with Jesus Christ, church is a drag. Nothing done in a worship service is exciting or like a party unless you understand what is going on.

The Party

People in Christ were as lost as any sheep or coin. They were the prodigal sons who had turned their backs on Jesus. They sowed their wild oats in a thousand distant lands and found out the hard way the truth of Jesus' words, "Apart from me you can do nothing" (John 15:5). And when they were sick and tired of being sick and tired, they woke up and came to their senses. They thought of Jesus and returned to recommit to him. And what did they find? Do you recall that twentieth verse?

He Ran to His Son

Can you even begin to comprehend that statement? As we turn around and head for home, God breaks into a dead run toward us. We don't deserve that kind of love, but that's what we get because that's the kind of God he is.

And God gives the *best* ring and the *best* robe, and he gives us sandals for our feet. He kills the fattened calf and throws a party in our honor. That's a description of the reception every sinner gets when he comes home to God. God extends forgiveness and restoration, he doesn't make you a slave. He wants sons and daughters. Church is a family reunion where the kids bask in the Father's love and where they love one another. A Sunday morning church gathering is a celebration of the Father's grace and mercy.

Sheep get lost through foolish choices. They don't hate the shepherd or the other sheep. They just wander off until they are lost and devoured by wolves. Coins get lost because of the carelessness of others. Boys get lost because they think they know more than the father. Older brothers get lost because of their pride. The important thing in these four stories is the value God places upon us as his poor lost sheep, lost coins, and lost sons and daughters.

CHAPTER TWENTY-FIVE

You Have Two Choices

You say, why didn't the father simply refuse to let the boy go? God knew it was best to give us the freedom of choice. God will not interfere with that. But we will have an eternity to live with the consequences of our choices.

Dear friend, you can choose to put Christ in your life or to leave him out. You can party now with celebrating Christians, and you can party in heaven with the redeemed of all ages. The party will never be over. God's way is simply the best way to live and the only way to die! This is your personal invitation to the party. Don't miss it. See you there!